ZERO HOUR FOR GEN X

HOW THE LAST ADULT
GENERATION CAN SAVE
AMERICA FROM MILLENNIALS

MATTHEW HENNESSEY

ENCOUNTER BOOKS
New York • London

First American edition published in 2018 by Encounter Books,
an activity of Encounter for Culture and Education, Inc.,
a nonprofit, tax exempt corporation.
Encounter Books website address: www.encounterbooks.com

Manufactured in the United States and printed on
acid-free paper. The paper used in this publication meets
the minimum requirements of ANSI/NISO Z39.48–1992
(R 1997) (*Permanence of Paper*).

FIRST AMERICAN EDITION

LIBRARY OF CONGRESS CATALOGING-IN-PUBLICATION DATA
Names: Hennessey, Matthew, 1973– author.
Title: Zero hour for gen X : how the last adult generation can save
America from millennials / by Matthew Hennessey.
Description: New York : Encounter Books, [2018] |
Includes bibliographical references and index.
Identifiers: LCCN 2018000152| ISBN 9781594039942 (hardcover : alk. paper) |
ISBN 9781594039959 (ebook)
Subjects: LCSH: Generation X—United States. | Intergenerational
communication—United States. | Intergenerational relations—
United States. | Conflict of generations—United States. |
Internet—Social aspects—United States.
Classification: LCC HQ799.7 .H475 2018 | DDC 305.2—dc23
LC record available at https://lccn.loc.gov/2018000152

Interior page design and composition: BooksByBruce.com

For my mother, who is surely smiling.

CONTENTS

INTRODUCTION

People generally remember the strapping actor Christopher Reeve for two things: his 1978 role as Superman and the unfortunate horseback-riding accident that left him paralyzed from the neck down in 1995. I remember him for something else.

Shortly before his accident, the Juilliard-trained Reeve gave a supple supporting performance in *The Remains of the Day* as an American congressman visiting the United Kingdom shortly before the outbreak of World War II. Anthony Hopkins and Emma Thompson took the starring roles, but Reeve's fine work in the melancholy Merchant Ivory drama was noticed and talked about. In a 1996 interview with Larry King, the wheelchair-bound Reeve said that he felt his accident had come just as he was poised to shake free of the action-hero persona that had clung to him since *Superman*. His career, he felt, was about to take a turn away from roles that required little more than that he look good. He was hoping to transition into substantive parts in better films.

"I was just getting the hang of it," he said with obvious regret.

After his accident, the once physically vital Reeve appeared in a handful of movies and did a bit of directing for television from his wheelchair, but physical paralysis robbed him of the opportunity to do what he'd worked so hard to prepare himself for. He died a few years later. The King interview added a layer of pathos to Reeve's tragic story. He lamented the loss of his power and athleticism, but what really bothered him was that he could never show the world what he was capable of doing as an actor.

This book is about Generation X, the relatively small cohort of Americans sandwiched between the twin generational behemoths known as the baby boomers and the millennials. Culturally, politically, socially, technologically, and economically, the torch is being passed from the older generation to the younger one while the one in the middle is being mostly ignored. With the baby boomers on the way out, the culture is turning its attention to millennial needs, millennial tastes, millennial peculiarities, and millennial preferences. Generation X is at best an afterthought—when we are thought of at all.[1]

My thesis is simple: if Generation X doesn't get its act together—and fast—we, like Christopher Reeve, will have the rug pulled out from under us just as we're on the verge of realizing our potential. That would be a pity, both for the individuals who could have made a difference and for a society that desperately needs a counterbalance to the millennial rush to a digital world, with its ethos of instant gratification, public shaming, and isolation-by-technology. In this new world, everything from privacy to freedom of speech is viewed as a relic from a boring, underdeveloped, and less enlightened past.

If you prefer newspapers and books to screens and pads; if your tastes run to music made with instruments rather than computers; if you value privacy; if you don't want behemoth tech firms spying on you in your home and your car, storing the data and selling it to the highest bidder so that you can be more accurately targeted by marketers and advertisers; if open debate is important to you and the chill winds of speech codes and political correctness on our college campuses have already sent a shiver up your spine; if saying what you like and laughing at what you find funny is your definition of freedom; if you'd rather work for a living than take a guaranteed government income financed by Silicon Valley profits; if drone deliveries and sex robots give you the creeps; if you've ever scratched your head in wonder after reading an article about what millennials know and how they think about the world—then this is the time to make a stand.

It is, as the title says, zero hour. Soon it'll be party over. Whoops! Out of time.

---

1 I thought long and hard about whether to refer to Generation X in the third person (they), or in the first (we). I opted to acknowledge my group membership and—for the most part—refer to Generation X as "us" and "we." As you will see, this is as much a memoir as it is history, social commentary, or policy proposal. If the habit unnerves you, I apologize, but I decided that I couldn't get away with pretending that the subjects discussed in these pages aren't deeply personal and informed by experience.

Not long ago I had a conversation with a woman who is younger than I am. I'm 44. I'd say she's about 25. I told her that I was working on finishing a book. She asked what it was about. I chose my words carefully.

"It's about Generation X," I said. She paused, a quizzical look on her face.

"Remind me who they are again?"

"They're people about my age, in our forties and early fifties," I told her. "It's about how we grew up in a world that was very different from the one that you and your friends grew up in and how that world is quickly slipping away."

"Great. Another book about how awful millennials are," she said. "Can't wait."

An understandable reaction; nobody wants to hear about the supposed shortcomings of a group that they had no choice but to join. I nodded dumbly and shrugged.

"Oh yeah, Generation X, I remember now," she said, flashing a wry smile. "You're the generation that isn't going to get a president."

"That's pretty much it," I had to concede.

This is the moment when members of Generation X should be setting the national agenda. We should be entering a period of social, political, and cultural influence, if not control. We have the experience and the energy necessary to do the big jobs. We should be getting ready to steer the ship, but we are about to get swamped by a millennial wave that has already started crashing hard into the worlds of business, politics, entertainment, religion, dating, medicine, and education. Even the military is watering down its once-rigid standards in order to cater to millennial penchants and predilections. If we don't act fast, the millennial wave is going to sweep Gen X overboard. We're going to miss our moment, becoming nothing more than a demographic footnote of American history—the inconsequential, shade-strewn valley wedged between two enormous generational peaks.

Raised in a pre-revolutionary moment technologically, Gen Xers are children of paper, pens, books, handshakes, body language, and eye contact. We learned the virtues of patience, self-control, and delayed gratification, even if we didn't always practice or appreciate them. We knew what it meant to be out of contact with someone we loved. Some of us, perhaps too few, learned how to fix an engine or wire a light fixture. Most remember how quiet things used to be; how easy it was to be alone.

Not so easy anymore, is it? Be honest.

America stands anxiously on the cusp of an unknown future. Unlike the baby boomers, Generation X's race is not yet run. Unlike the millennials, we remember what life was like before the Internet invaded and conquered nearly everything. In that memory resides the hope of our collective redemption, the seed of a renewal that could stem the rot, decay, erosion, and collapse all around us. If that seems overly dramatic or impossibly grandiose, well, all I can say is this is my book, not yours. I'm not going to all this trouble because I think the stakes are low or the future is already written.

Gen Xers can write our own future; there's still time for that.

ONE

The Baby Boom and Everything After

In early 2017, Maxine Waters, a 13-term Democratic congresswoman from southern California, gave a short speech during a panel discussion of so-called "net neutrality" rules—the bewilderingly complex regulatory regime then governing Internet service providers that has since been repealed. The topic remains of seemingly great importance to the young, idealistic, hip, and tech savvy. Rep. Waters is none of those things. She is pushing 80, a feisty partisan, more than a little cynical about the prospect of working fruitfully with members of the other major political party, and—this is just a guess—she doesn't really understand how the Internet works.

It's not a knock; few 80-year-olds know how the Internet works. For that matter, not many 40-year-olds or 20-year-olds know how the mysterious, detached, electronic, networked brain that increasingly dominates our every waking moment actually works. We think we know. We have an idea, maybe, but we probably couldn't articulate it in a way that would add up to much. It could be a cloud. It could be tubes. Whatever it is, it's complicated, to borrow a popular phrase from the social media revolution. For most of us, that's about all we can reliably say about the Internet—it's complicated.

On this particular day, the congresswoman was unconcerned with all that complexity. She was talking to a roomful of true believers—tech people, the best of the best, the elite thinkers, makers, and doers in our economy. In her enthusiasm to demonstrate how committed she was to whatever they were committed to, Rep. Waters got carried away.

"Our millennials are a force," she said. "And I was a millennial once, too. No longer, of course. But I love what you're doing."

She was a millennial once?

Rep. Waters's curious remark got some attention, mostly in the conservative Twittersphere, where she is often a target, both for her outspoken progressivism and for her frequent political grandstanding on cable TV. Right-wing tweeters went after her this time not for demanding the impeachment of Donald Trump, which was almost her daily ritual at the time, but for transparently pandering to a millennial audience (which, by the way, she didn't need to do—they already adored her). Her awkward phrasing could perhaps have been chalked up to a slip of the tongue. We know what she meant by it, after all. But it was so politically pathetic it can't be ignored, even if you side with her and not with the right-wing Internet jackals.

Rep. Waters's remark was characteristic of the current cultural obsession with the millennial generation. Everywhere you turn the questions are the same: What do they want? How do they think? How should we change the world to suit what they want and how they think? How can we make them love us? When will they realize how powerful their size makes them as a voting and consuming bloc? How can we influence their habits and preferences before they realize that they're bigger than we are and that the American experiment will eventually belong to them?

The congresswoman's millennial suck-up was a neat illustration of the desperation with which the aging members of the baby boom have sought to cling to relevance.[1] It astonishes. It shouldn't, at this late date, but it does. No previous generation has continued dressing like children this far into old age. No previous generation has so ardently insisted on refusing to grow up. The baby boomers are something new under the American sun: elderly people who listen to music made for teenagers

---

[1] Maxine Waters is not, strictly speaking, a baby boomer. She got herself out of the gate just slightly ahead of that generational stampede.

and adamantly insist on having their own way all the time. They are a generational wrecking ball in baseball caps and t-shirts. They famously have no regard for anyone's needs but their own.

If it sounds familiar, it should. The millennials and the baby boomers are cut from the same cloth.

Nobody wakes up in the morning and sees a generation in the mirror. We're all individuals. We all have unique personalities formed by a churning bouillabaisse of mysterious genetic and environmental influences. These include the circumstances into which we were born and the manner in which we were brought up. They include our parents' abilities and personalities, the region of the country we lived in as children, and even perhaps the dynamics of the business and economic cycle at play during our formative years.

Many streams feed the ocean; many trees compose the forest. We are all something special. We are all just us.

A lot of people say the concept of discrete generations is so fuzzy that there's no point in using it as a lens through which to analyze political, cultural, social, and economic trends. As if tens of millions of people could possibly be of one mind, or even similar minds, about important matters. I see the logic. It seems silly on the face of it to assume that an American born in 1965 would have the same attitudes and opinions as someone born in 1980, but they are likely to share at least a common vocabulary, as University of California, Berkeley, political scientist Laura Stoker notes, "by virtue of having experienced a specific set of social, economic, technological, and/or political circumstances at a formative period in their lives."

Still don't buy it? If you're a Gen Xer, ask a millennial if she knows who Christa McAuliffe was, what night of the week *Cheers* was on, or what breakfast cereal Mikey liked. These answers will likely be on the tip of your tongue but will leave millennials staring blankly at their avocado toast. If you're a millennial, try the same trick on a baby boomer. Ask him how to use Venmo, or what a Snapstreak is, or whether Ron Weasley was Ravenclaw, Slytherin, Hufflepuff, or Gryffindor. You will be forced to conclude that all non-millennials are muggles. Your generational affiliation provides you with the grammar, the syntax, and the context necessary to understand and interpret events. It's your native tongue.

I offer a simple premise: viewing the world through the lens of generations is neither more nor less legitimate than viewing it through the lenses of gender, race, class, education level, immigration status, sexual preference, criminal history, political affiliation—or any of the other general descriptive categories that journalists, politicians, and social scientists use to try to explain the past and predict the future. We accept that understanding election results requires us to break down the voting population into categories such as "black women," "retirees," or "working-class whites." While it should be self-evident that black women aren't of one mind politically or that working-class whites in West Virginia have different priorities than those in Florida or Oregon, we use the categories nonetheless because they help organize our thinking about the electorate and provide a jumping-off point for larger discussions about why we vote the way we do. This, in turn, helps us understand who we are, what we want, and where we're going as a nation. Though we remain individuals, these broad frames are the conceptual tools available to us, and it's not clear what better alternatives exist.

The parameters defining the three generations that concern me are approximate. For the purposes of clarity, I will spell them out. Baby boomers are those born roughly between 1946 and 1964. Generation Xers are those born roughly between 1965 and 1980. The millennials are those born roughly between 1981 and 1997. In 2015, according to Pew Research Center, there were 75.4 million millennials, 74.9 million baby boomers, and 66 million Gen Xers in the United States. Even as they are dying out, there are still 9 million more baby boomers than there are Gen Xers. The millennials are already the largest American generation, and they're still growing due to immigration. Pew estimates a peak millennial population of 81 million by 2036.

To reiterate, these definitions can seem loose, and individuals often confound stereotypes. There is a lot of give in the generational idea. I know there are baby boomers who love SoundCloud rap, Gen Xers who listen to Frank Sinatra (unironically), and millennials with old souls.

"Generational boundaries are fuzzy, arbitrary, and culture-driven," acknowledge Paul Taylor and George Gao in a 2014 Pew study of Generation X, but "once fixed by the mysterious forces of the zeitgeist, they tend to firm up over time." That's what I'm aiming to capture here when I make broad claims about the generations: a sense of the cultural, economic, and social dynamics at work during the formative years of people who were born around the same time, and how those dynamics have influenced that cohort's collective interpretation of events, trends, and outcomes.

*   *   *

The baby boom produced a generation that nearly destroyed America. The cohort that went from Woodstock to Wall Street squandered an inheritance of liberty unique in the history of the world. Through endless protest, non-negotiable demands, and an overweening disregard for the values and mores of the pragmatic, sacrificial, citizen-soldier generation that raised them, the baby boomers took a good thing—midcentury America[2]—and basically blew it. In Europe and Asia, the baby boomers' parents had seen and participated in slaughter and sacrifice on a historically unprecedented scale. Those who survived came home looking for a way to live that paid tribute to the dead friends they had left behind overseas. They wanted peaceful and quiet lives. They aspired to comfort and prosperity. They sought security. For some reason this irked the baby boomers, who looked at their parents and saw not "the greatest generation" but the most uptight one. They interpreted their parents' desire for tranquil conformity not as the natural reaction to a season of war but as a kind of bloodless conservatism bent on sapping young people of the joy in being alive.

The baby boom was an anomaly, the result of a unique confluence of circumstances and events that is unlikely ever to be repeated. Fertility rates in the United States declined steadily throughout the late 19th century and into the first decades of the 20th century. The outbreak of World War II essentially removed millions of husbands and fathers from the domestic marriage market. When the soldiers came home at war's end, the pent-up demand for love, marriage, and the baby carriage sent birthrates skyward. Jobs were plentiful and wages were rising. Credit to buy suburban housing was easy to acquire. Thanks to the GI Bill, higher education was within easy reach of returning soldiers in ways that it wasn't for young men and women prior to the war.

"The space and income for providing for more children was now available," according to Columbia University history professor Herbert S. Klein, "and Americans responded to these opportunities by lowering

---

2 I didn't say it was a perfect thing, I said it was a good thing. It may even have been a great thing, but I know that it's a hot topic, so I'll stop at good.

the age at which they married, beginning their families at an earlier age, and opting for marriage more frequently, thus increasing their overall fertility."

The baby boom was on. In 1946, 3.4 million children were born in the United States, a 20 percent spike from the year before. Seventy-six million Americans were born between 1946 and 1964. These new Americans were born into a country experiencing unprecedented prosperity. While most of the rest of the world spent the 1950s trying to put their broken countries back together after the devastation of World War II, the good ole U.S. of A. was booming like a thunderclap under Presidents Harry S. Truman and Dwight D. Eisenhower. Overall, the economy grew nearly 40 percent larger during the course of the decade. Unemployment was low, productivity was high, gas was cheap, cars and televisions were affordable, and time-saving household appliances added hours of leisure to the day. All in all, it was a great time to be born and a great place to be born in.

It wasn't all rosy for everyone. In parts of the South, Jim Crow laws and de facto racial segregation kept African-Americans from participating fully in society, almost a hundred years after the end of the Civil War. This was a historical wrong on its way to being righted—but it must be noted early and emphatically in any social history of the era. Some Americans missed out on the dream. Because of the color of their skin, people's lives were not as realized as they could have been. It was nothing short of a human tragedy and a stain on the nation's good name.

Still, even for poor African-Americans in the South and elsewhere, a booming economy had a transformative effect on Americans' lives. The post-war economic miracle wasn't a straight-line ride. A recession in 1960–61 led President Kennedy in 1963 to cut taxes, causing the economy again to take off like a rocket. Year-over-year GDP growth was in the 5 percent range throughout the decade. By 1970, the average American felt 50 percent richer than he had in 1960. That's an experience that few American generations have ever had, or likely ever will have again. The baby boomers had been dealt a straight flush, and then another, and then another—nothing but blue skies from here to the horizon. Perhaps it gave them a false sense of how easy the game of life would be to play. It may have convinced them that the fair winds would blow forever no matter how badly they sailed or how hard they tried to scuttle the ship.

Despite the abundance of peace and prosperity during their teenage years and early adulthood, or perhaps because of it, the baby boomers went to war against American institutions and values. They fought as if their cause carried with it the Mandate of Heaven. Whether on campus, in the streets, or around the family dinner table, idealistic baby boomers took their righteous fight straight to "the man" in all his capitalistic, militaristic, and bourgeois guises. In economics and global affairs they did much the same thing, breaking rules, smashing norms, and generally behaving as if they alone had been selected to rid God's green earth of tired convention and shabby conformity.

We know the details of their story like we know the letters of the alphabet, in part because the baby boomers haven't stopped patting themselves on the back since Dylan went electric. From *Easy Rider* to *The Big Chill* and from "For What It's Worth" to "We Didn't Start the Fire," Generation X stood patiently by as the Woodstock generation constructed endless monuments to their own "achievements."[3] On the plinth of each is inscribed: We Built This City on Rock 'n' Roll.

The Democratic political operative Paul Begala once called baby boomers a "garbage barge" of a generation. "Guys who once dropped acid are now downing VIAGRA; women who once eschewed lipstick are now getting liposuction," he wrote contemptuously of his own age cohort in *Esquire* way back in April 2000. "I know it's a sin to hate, so let me put it this way: If [baby boomers] were animals, they'd be a plague of locusts, devouring everything in their path and leaving but a wasteland." He went on to compare baby boomers to kudzu—the invasive climbing weed—as well as to shortsighted abstract expressionists and to the Florida Marlins, who won the 1997 World Series with an assemblage of well-paid mercenaries and free agents who were promptly sold off to the highest bidder.

"Garbage barge," I must say, has an irresistible assonant lilt, though it's a bit of a harsh tag to lay on a group of 75 million–odd people, some of whom are currently in their seventies. While the oldest of the baby boomers, including many of their cultural and countercultural heroes, have begun cashing out, the youngest boomers are just now hitting

---

3 Billy Joel said they didn't start the fire, but I've always felt that was an awfully defensive way of putting it. If you didn't actually start the fire, people will believe you. The truth will come out. Protesting so loudly and frequently seems an obvious, and pathetic, way of signaling that you in fact *did* start the fire but fear all of the credit will somehow go to someone else.

retirement age. Barack Obama is in some key ways their last lion—the youngest, purest distillation of their utopian ethos. But even the former president is not exiting the pool as he should. Like so many of the baby boomers, he seems intent on hanging around longer than is seemly. Donald Trump might be the last baby boomer in the Oval Office, but even if he isn't, this garbage barge's domination of the country's social, political, and economic life must come to a natural end eventually.

The baby boomers will leave an identifiable legacy, though it isn't necessarily the one they'd hoped for back in the heady days of yesteryear.[4] Instead of the beautiful trail of peace, love, freedom, and understanding that they aspired to carve from the American jungle of imperfect justice, their contribution at the moment looks more like a litany of endless war, sky-high debt, hyper-partisanship, and cultural decay. Their dream of peace and harmony gave way to the nightmare of a diseased political culture, where every election is potentially the end of the world and where it's almost always mandatory to impugn the other guy's motives. At first they wouldn't trust anyone over 30. Then the threshold was raised to 40. They kept revising it upward until there was no one left not to trust but themselves, which, judging from the tribal political drift of the past 20 years, they don't.

As they aged, the baby boomers turned pissy and started insisting, against all available evidence, that they were leaving the place the way they had found it. *No!* That's not giving them enough credit for their relentless boosterism. America was *better* than when they'd found it, they argued: more just, less corrupt, kinder, gentler, and in touch with its feelings and faults.

The boomers won't leave a vacuum when they go, if they ever actually do go. The young-and-hungry millennials are ready to pounce. At almost 80 million strong, these tech-savvy up-and-comers are conspiring even as I write to seize the commanding heights of the economy and culture. If "conspiring" seems too strong a word, you maybe haven't been paying attention to the interplanetary ambitions of Silicon Valley's "visionary" set. Consider, too, how forcefully and effectively the millennial generation has expressed itself in successive street and campus protests in support of Occupy Wall Street, Black Lives Matter, Antifa, and the anti-Trump

---

4 You know, back when Maxine Waters was a millennial.

"resistance." Millennials are politically engaged, culturally demanding, and commercially powerful. They are not used to being told "no." They are not used to being asked to wait their turn. They are the direct-message generation. Nobody should expect them to put in 20 to 30 years before being offered positions of responsibility and influence, the way previous generations did. Even the baby boomers, crazy as they were, played by those rules. Millennials will burn the place down first.

But before we get to all that, what about Generation X? The under-sized group of Americans sandwiched between the baby boomers and the millennials was once considered a potent cultural force. Roughly 65 million Americans—including yours truly—came of age in the 1980s and 1990s and are now somewhere between the ages of 37 and 52. The oldest among us remember Watergate as children, along with a bunch of other signal events and characters of the 1970s—Bruce Jenner, gas lines, the Wide World of Sports, Ayatollah Khomeini. Now we are in mid-career and heading toward mid-life. Some have begun paying for our own kids to go to college. Many are deep into 30-year mortgages. A few are even looking ahead to retirement.

Although we are still in the middle innings, it feels like we've seen it all. We've lived through recessions, rebounds, and riots. We've seen wars—a number of them. As teenagers, we gaped at the collapse of communism and the reordering of the international system. In our teens and early twenties, we reveled in prosperity at home and peace abroad. We witnessed a presidential impeachment and the dawning of a new millennium. As we hurtled toward our thirties, finding our mates and starting our families, Islamic terrorism reached our shores. The darkest day, September 11, 2001, forced us to face the cold reality of living in an unfriendly world. As we started buying homes and saving for the future, the bottom fell out of the global economy.

There has been an upside to living in what can only be called inter-esting times. Owing to a set of social, political, cultural, and economic forces entirely beyond our control, Gen X was brought up in a way that was different from the generation that followed. We were raised on ana-log technology—pencils, pens, notepads, books, index cards, the Dewey Decimal System, newspapers, magazines, back issues, posters, mail order (sorry, no COD), records and record players, cassette tapes and boom boxes, video stores, landline telephones, answering machines, beepers, radios with dials, televisions with rabbit ears, static, cameras with film inside them, muscle cars with engines that a teenager could learn to fix, maps, atlases, encyclopedias, the Sears catalog, cigarette machines, Zippo lighters, bank tellers, passbooks, stamp collections, and cold hard cash money.

We weren't issued iPads in kindergarten. In fact, many of our elementary school desks still had inkwells in them in the 1970s. We were the last to take wood shop, metal shop, and home economics classes; we were the first to take "computers." We had snapshot cameras but we never photographed our meals or ourselves in bathroom mirrors. We never sent each other nude instant messages. Because HIV and AIDS were on the march during the late 1980s, we learned the dangers of sexual promiscuity in school. We were taught that there are only two genders, because no one had yet dreamed up a different paradigm.

Generation X comes from a tactile world that in some corners of America has already disappeared. We rode bicycles without helmets on our heads or pads on our elbows. We walked to school, baseball practice, play rehearsal, and home again—all unsupervised. We roamed our neighborhoods until the sun set. We climbed trees and jumped off garage roofs. We rode buses alone and waited in parked cars with the windows cracked and the doors locked while our parents went grocery shopping. For the most part we managed not to get kidnapped, killed, lost, or badly injured. Nobody called the cops when they saw us alone and minding our own business. When it was absolutely necessary that we get in touch with our parents—or our friends—we somehow managed to do it without cell phones. All of this independence equipped us with resilience and self-reliance, characteristics that have slowly been going missing in America. One need only reference the burgeoning literature on how to foster grit in children to get the picture.

Generation X was conditioned to accept that hard work should—and would—be rewarded, and that, in many if not most cases, honest labor was its own reward. From the teachers, coaches, neighbors, and parents who formed us, we learned that it was a lucky thing to be born an American. It was something to be glad about and to defend if necessary. For all America's well-documented faults, it's still the shining city on a hill. It's still the place that the world's tired, hungry, and poor dream of reaching. We are still the last, best hope. That's what we were taught.

Now, during our summer years, the American experiment has been irradiated by the unstable particles let loose by the political fission of the Trump presidency. Precisely what health effects on our democracy will derive from prolonged exposure to these populist isotopes is as yet impossible to predict. But the social landscape is mutating, and has been for two decades. The culture that once buffeted us is eroding. The economic conditions that enriched our grandparents and sustained our parents are stagnating. We haven't done as well or gone as far as recent generations did. We see cracks beginning to form in the great edifice of American tradition and continuity. Nothing seems like what it was anymore. Nothing seems like it will be what we thought it would be. Everything feels like it's on the verge of radical change, or complete collapse.

Generation X has a lot to give, but a roiling country doesn't seem much interested in our contributions at the moment. There are some who say that when England's nonagenarian monarch Queen Elizabeth II dies, the throne should pass not to Prince Charles, her septuagenarian son, but to Prince William, her thirtysomething grandson. That's the kind of injustice that Generation X faces—a jumping of the queue. I'm no fan of monarchy, but it seems only fair that the fellow who has dutifully waited his turn for 70 years should at least get his shot at the title. He's earned it. He seems up to it. The guy who's next in line may appear to be the more attractive candidate—young, vital, in touch with the now—but the rules are the rules. They ought to be, anyway. They used to be.

Before Generation X gets made redundant, I'd like to see us make a last stand.

TWO

Watching the World Wake Up from History

I f Generation X is to save America, it has to first understand what makes it so special. That's a tough assignment, because Gen Xers were raised to believe that we weren't terribly special. When we lost Little League games and swim meets, we went home without trophies or medals. Our parents told us that defeat done properly was character building, a lesson we've absorbed and that for most of us has paid dividends in our professional careers and personal relationships. There were few, if any, taboos in place about telling kids the truth in the 1970s and '80s. If you were bad at something, you were likely to find out about it, and in pretty short order. The Cult of Constant Encouragement had not yet formed. "Wait until the Army gets a hold of you" was one of my dad's favorite sayings when, as a teenager, I was being lazy, insouciant, disrespectful, or, as was frequently the case, all three.[5]

---

5 The Army never did manage to get a hold of me, though many of my high school classmates who ended up in uniform emerged as fully formed adults in their mid-twenties—a time when I was still sleeping until noon and whining about having to work to support myself. I briefly contemplated joining the military after 9/11 but had only just fallen in love with the woman who would become my wife. I couldn't bear the thought of leaving her. A few years later I applied to join the NYPD, going so far as to sit for the entrance exam for the police academy at Washington Irving High School near Union Square. The timing wasn't right then, either. We had a new baby

Sometime around 1985, the term "slacker" entered my vocabulary and that of my teenage friends. I know where it came from—Robert Zemeckis's blockbuster time-travel comedy *Back to the Future* starring the then twentysomething superstar Michael J. Fox as the fast-talking wiseacre high-school kid Marty McFly. Like celluloid teens from Andy Hardy to Ferris Bueller, McFly had a lot more going on outside school than in it. This naturally put him on the outs with Hill Valley High principal Gerald Strickland, played by the bald-headed character actor James Tolkan. Anytime McFly stepped foot into Hill Valley's hallway, he managed to step wrong with his nemesis.

"You got a real attitude problem, McFly," barks Principal Strickland one morning after issuing Marty a tardy slip accompanied by a sharp finger to the chest. "You're a slacker. You remind me of your father when he went here. He was a slacker, too."

Tolkan played Strickland perfectly as the no-nonsense drill sergeant that many male school administrators of the 1980s actually once had been. These big-chested principals and vice principals of the so-called greatest generation, who had been to war in Europe, the Pacific, and Korea, were responsible for maintaining discipline in many of the schools that Gen Xers attended. They did it by prowling the hallways, scowling, and occasionally letting loose their big, booming voices. I well remember one— Mr. Brody—giving a cafeteria of 10-year-olds a dressing down so bullish that it would have embarrassed General Patton. Mr. Brody warned that if our bad behavior didn't end, "Heads will roll!" He wasn't punning—he meant to threaten us. It was his famous catchphrase and he punctuated it with a bash of his beefy closed fist atop a metal cafeteria dishwasher. The effect was like the cannon in the finale of the *1812 Overture*.

I'm as sure that Mr. Brody's performance brought a swift and certain end to the cafeteria shenanigans as I am that such a bravura turn would get the poor man arrested—or virally shamed—in 2018. My father told me years later that Mr. Brody had been a Marine during World War II. He'd seen action at Guadalcanal, Bougainville, and Guam. He was the big cheese at the local VFW and American Legion posts in our town,

and my wife was understandably concerned about the danger of the job. One thing led to another and I ended up working on the editorial page of the *Wall Street Journal*, so things probably ended up the way they were supposed to for me. Still, I often think that had I been half a man, I would have marched right down to the recruiter's office in Times Square and joined up on September 12. I was only 27. They could have used me, I'm sure, had they been able to get a hold of me.

a genuine American hero and a pillar of the community. I wonder: do such men go into elementary education anymore?

Among the reasons Gen X never felt special was baby boomers' constant insistence that everything good, true, pure, and worthwhile had already taken place back in the 1960s, a decade that never really ended for those who lived through it. The glorious spirit of the '60s stretched on through the '70s and into the '80s thanks to the baby boomers' unlimited capacity for self-congratulation. During the '80s, every 20-year anniversary of every minor Age of Aquarius milestone was marked with a two-hour television special or a commemorative issue of *LIFE* magazine. Many of the more consequential historical events and personalities were turned into blockbuster movies. The Kennedy assassination, the Civil Rights Movement, Malcolm X, the British Invasion, the Doors, RFK, the Hippies, the Yippies, the '68 Democratic Convention, Nixon, Woodstock, the space race and the moon landing—they all got the soft-focus treatment.

And then there was Vietnam.

Gen Xers never stopped hearing about it. We read books and short stories about it in high school English class. The newspapers were filled with debates about monuments and parades for the war's mistreated veterans. We saw an endless stream of movies about the war on the weekends—*Good Morning, Vietnam*; *Full Metal Jacket*; *Platoon*; *Born on the Fourth of July*; *Casualties of War*; *Uncommon Valor*. Even Rambo, the muscle-bound survivalist played by Sylvester Stallone in a string of highly successful action flicks, was a Vietnam vet. Gen X listened to music about the Vietnam War, music inspired by it, and music made during it because radio stations in the 1970s and '80s still mostly played music that baby boomers wanted to hear. With a few exceptions, mainstream radio stations didn't care about the music my friends and I liked. Unless you were lucky enough to live near a college with its own call sign, most of the time you had to settle for stations playing the "classic rock" favored by people then in their thirties, forties, and fifties—the Beatles, the Rolling Stones, Janis Joplin, the Who, Eric Clapton, Led Zeppelin.

Throughout most of the '80s Gen X had to go to MTV to hear music that wasn't two decades old, but even the fledgling music video channel got swept up in '60s throwback mania. One of its weirder on-air personalities was a guy called "Randee of the Redwoods," a hippie-dippy space cadet who introduced videos while wearing tie-dye headbands and purple tinted sunglasses. One of my favorite programs in junior high school was "The Monkees," a madcap musical comedy about an imaginary four-piece rock band that first aired in 1966 and was resurrected by MTV in 1986. It got to the point where the '60s seemed so familiar to Gen X, it was almost as if we'd been there. We wore tie-dye t-shirts and decorated our college dorm rooms with lava lamps, Jimi Hendrix posters, and other '60s bric-a-brac. We knew that decade's history, personalities, anxieties, and psychological quirks better than we knew our own.

In reality, Gen Xers *did* have our own personality and psychology. It was just that the long shadow of the baby boom occasionally made them hard to discern. In hindsight, the environmental forces that shaped Gen X seem much clearer. A series of signal events stand out: the bicentennial of 1976, the fall of the Berlin Wall, the Rodney King riots, the O. J. Simpson trial, the Clinton impeachment, and the terrorist attacks of September 11, 2001. Each in its own way molded the Gen X worldview. Each played a part in forming the Gen X character.

The bicentennial celebrations of 1976 are for many Gen Xers the earliest memory they have of being American. Streets and homes that summer were festooned with flags and bunting. Fireworks and picnics, brass bands and Uncle Sam hats, pageantry and patriotism—it was a unique and compelling moment. The country was exhausted by the baby boomers' extended teenage rebellion, Watergate, the Nixon resignation, and the humiliating surrender in Vietnam. The bicentennial was a much-needed national party that came right on time.

Nineteen seventy-six was also an election year, and that November Americans selected Georgia's Democratic governor, Jimmy Carter, as their 39th president. For the next four years, the country underwent an extended existential crisis. The oldest members of Generation X—then between the ages of about 10 and 15—had a front-row seat.

Throughout the late '70s, the American economy stagnated even as the cost of essential items rose higher and higher. In 1979, according to the Federal Reserve Bank of Minneapolis, the consumer price index—a measure of the average change over time of a set of goods and services—spiked 11.3 percent for the year. In 1980 and 1981, CPI continued to rise by 13.5 and 10.3 percent, respectively. The combination of low growth and high inflation occasioned a new and unwieldy coinage—stagflation. Oil shocks and embargoes sent Americans out in the middle of the night to form lines at gas stations. Cars themselves started transforming from big, bulky, metal gas guzzlers into lean, mean, fuel-efficient hatchbacks. President Carter addressed the nation in February 1977, suggesting that high prices and low growth would be the new normal in America.

"[I]f we all cooperate and make modest sacrifices, if we learn to live thriftily and remember the importance of helping our neighbors, then we can find ways to adjust and to make our society more efficient, and our own lives more enjoyable and productive," he said. Gen X was formed in an environment of scarcity.

Times were tough in the late '70s, and the culture reflected it. The nation's once-great big cities were tumbling into crime, disorder, and political dysfunction. Fashion trends and tastes were drifting toward the gritty. Movies and television detailed the underbelly of life in places like graffiti-plagued New York and smog-smothered Los Angeles. America started to get that rundown look. Where once the entertainment culture focused on the upbeat and the positive, things started taking a darker turn. The glamorous aspects of society weren't spared; they, too, seemed haunted by fear and decay—*Saturday Night Fever*, *Columbo*, *Sanford and Son*, even the droids in *Star Wars* were beat-up and rusty.

It wasn't Hollywood fiction; all was not well. Child and grown-up alike could feel it. Over everything in the 1970s lurked the constant threat of nuclear annihilation. The Soviet Union was expanding its borders, testing the West's commitment to the long-standing policy of containment. In 1979, the Soviet Army invaded Afghanistan, a historically unconquerable Muslim nation known to students of history as The Place Where Empires Go to Die. Alexander the Great, Genghis Khan, and the British East India Company all tried and failed to pacify the land beyond the Hindu Kush. In 1979 kids like me who sat on the couch as their parents watched the *CBS Evening News* with Walter Cronkite couldn't have imagined that words like "mujahedeen" and "jihad" would still be in our ears and on the tips of our tongues nearly 40 years later.

At the same time Soviet power seemed to be expanding, America's world footprint seemed to be shrinking. Also in 1979, the Shah of Iran—an extravagantly corrupt American client—was deposed by a radical Islamic revolution led by the Paris-based Shia cleric Ayatollah Ruhollah Khomeini. With Khomeini's blessing, Islamic student radicals took 52

American diplomats and citizens hostage in Tehran and held them for more than a year. A rescue attempt by the U.S. Military in April 1980 failed miserably. Helicopters carrying the Army's elite special operators (aka Delta Force) were foiled by desert sands, and the mission was called off. In the confusion of the retreat, one of the helicopters crashed into a transport aircraft containing jet fuel. Eight soldiers were killed. The mission—dubbed Operation Eagle Claw—was a complete disaster. "America's elite rescue force had lost eight men, seven helicopters, and a C-130, and had not even made contact with the enemy. It was a debacle," wrote Mark Bowden in the *Atlantic*. "It defined the word 'debacle.'"

Coming off the dreadful surrender in Vietnam, America was again on the back foot, projecting ineptitude, impotence, and weakness to the world. Most Gen Xers were too young to gain more than an atmospheric sense of the times, but that's often what childhood is. The zeitgeist as we understood it was that American power was fragile. We were vulnerable, and possibly on the cusp of a humbling national decline. Khomeini was an archvillain, made to order for a generation that woke up early on Saturday mornings to watch cartoons on TV.

I recall Jimmy Carter, the guy who was allegedly going to protect us from such baddies, only as the gentle old man in an orange cardigan who spoke with a hypnotically pleasing Southern drawl. I occasionally saw him on Cronkite, which my dad never missed during those years. The man I thought of as President Mister Rogers lost the White House to Ronald Reagan in 1980, a few weeks after my seventh birthday. Reagan seemed to project a different image than President Carter. He was jaunty and vital. He smiled and joked. His hair shined. Even though I was young, and a member of a staunchly Democratic family, the changing of the guard wasn't lost on me. Maybe we were going to be all right after all.

The oldest Gen Xers were entering high school during the waning years of the 1970s, and their impressions of the era are better drawn than mine. To them, it was a time of youthful innocence: banana-seat bikes and Evel Knievel stunts; Muhammad Ali prize fights and *Welcome Back, Kotter* characters; Andy Gibb, disco, Peter Frampton, *Charlie's Angels*, and Fat Albert. It was a time when childhood was still a little bit risky. No one dreamed of wearing a helmet while riding a bike. Seat belts were optional. Pizza parlors had cigarette machines in the corner, and no adult would ever take time out of the day to wag a finger at a bunch of high school kids as they puffed away, cursing loudly, drinking soda and carrying on. Parenting then was a hands-off job. So was being a neighbor. Kids as young as I was left the house on summer mornings, only coming back to be fed at midday and dinnertime. We all were gullible enough to believe that mixing Pop Rocks and soda could kill you.

Most members of Generation X became socially and politically aware during the Reagan, Bush 41, and Clinton years, a time of growing economies and relative global and domestic peace. For most of the 1980s and '90s, the American economy hummed like a Harley engine, offering Generation X the tantalizing prospect of a richer, more materially secure life than their parents had led—and, the late 1970s aside, their parents had led relatively rich and materially secure lives. Between the beginning of the Reagan boom in 1983 and the epoch-defining year of 2001, the gross domestic product of the United States increased 81 percent in inflation-adjusted terms. The median household income of middle-class Americans grew by 25 percent during the same period. It was a good time to enter the job market. "If you can't get a job in this economy, there's something wrong with you," my mother said to me as I was out looking for a part-time job during the mid-'90s.

Not everyone experienced rising standards of living during the '80s and '90s. The 1987 stock market crash, the bursting of the dot-com bubble in the late 1990s, and periodic recessions such as the 1991–92 slowdown that gave rise to James Carville's famous "It's the economy, stupid" line caused real—though limited—economic pain. In the main, however, the United States was more prosperous than it had ever been. This is the economic reality that produced Generation X: we've seen the good and we've seen the bad. We know that we are in no way entitled to live in a prosperous and growing world. Such things aren't written in the stars. The choices we make matter.

Looking outward from America's shores, Gen X was the last generation to experience the drama and anxiety of the prospect of a nuclear conflict with the Soviet Union. Like our parents before us, we lived under the shadow of The Bomb. Movies like *The Day After*, *Red Dawn*, and *The Hunt for Red October* dramatized the conflict and made us hope that the coldhearted commies liked blue jeans and rock 'n' roll more than they loved the idea of global thermonuclear war. "I hope the Russians love their children, too," sang Sting. Yet, miracle of miracles, the Cold

War ended right before our eyes. We woke up one morning to learn that the Berlin Wall—the very symbol of oppression, authoritarianism, and despair—had fallen. It seems silly now, in this age of radical and constant connectivity, the idea of a concrete wall with razor wire on top separating two halves of a single global city. In hindsight it seems like it was never going to last, that it was foreordained that the wall would come down.

Trust me, it wasn't. In 1986 the Berlin Wall had as bright a future as the Great Wall of China—until it didn't. Nothing is written.

Hard on the heels of the celebrations in Berlin, the Soviet Union itself collapsed, mostly of its own weight, to be replaced by a federation of nominally democratic republics. The good guys had won. The bad guys had lost. Freedom was on the march. Liberty was in the air. The political scientist Francis Fukuyama declared it "the end of history."

Generation X entered its young adulthood with the expectation of inheriting a world at peace, a *Pax Americana* enforced by the unprecedented global supremacy of the U.S. Military. It was the dawn, in President George H. W. Bush's infamous term, of a "new world order." While that particular construction struck some as ominous at the time (it sounded like a global cabal of secret power), it was meant to convey that a paradigm shift in international relations had taken place—and it had. The old order of a bipolar world headed for mutually assured destruction had loomed over our parents' lives, and to some extent our own, but was suddenly, gloriously swept away. The country that young Americans called home was now the biggest, toughest kid on the block. Many considered it the dawn of a new, democratic, and peaceful era. Anything seemed possible.

All was not quiet, however, especially on the racial front. Race relations in America had seemed relatively tranquil throughout most of the 1980s. The sense was that the racial problems plaguing American communities in the 1960s and '70s had been worked out. A détente reigned. Tens of millions of Americans tuned in to NBC on Thursday nights at 8 p.m. to watch *The Cosby Show*. The challenges faced by Dr. Cliff Huxtable and his upper middle-class African-American family were no different, it seemed, from those faced by the middle-class white families depicted on *Happy Days* or *The Brady Bunch*. In fact, the Huxtables were funnier, more relatable. *The Cosby Show*'s multi-racial spinoff, *A Different World*, starring Sinbad and Lisa Bonet, was a hit with young white audiences, too.

Suburban white kids were learning to love rap music as they devoured after-school programming like *Yo! MTV Raps*. Jesse Jackson mounted a credible bid for the Democratic nomination for president in 1988.

Because the entertainment culture was seemingly integrated and color-blind, many white members of Generation X concluded that America was a post-racial society. It wasn't. In the early 1990s, several high-profile crimes exposed America's still-deep and still-festering racial divide. In March 1991, a group of Los Angeles police officers were caught on a grainy video beating 25-year-old Rodney King following a high-speed freeway chase. An African-American who was driving drunk, King later said that he fled from the cops out of fear that he was in violation of parole related to a previous robbery conviction. The officers struck him with a Taser. On the video, King could be seen repeatedly attempting to stand up and lunging toward officers. The officers tried to subdue him with baton blows and kicks. On tape, the whole thing looked like the savage beat-down that it was. The outnumbered King appeared to plead for mercy as the LAPD cops took turns shellacking him. From the distance that the video was filmed, it seemed like they were doing it for sport.

King ended up with broken bones in his face and ankle, and multiple other injuries. Relations between the LAPD and the city's black community were already at the breaking point, thanks to the city's long-standing gang problem and some serious corruption and abuse on the part of the cops. The video sparked nationwide outrage and led to the arrest of four of the officers involved. They testified at trial that King had ignored their repeated instructions to stop resisting and that they followed appropriate procedures. A 12-person Ventura County jury composed of 10 whites and no African-Americans agreed that the police had done nothing wrong, acquitting the officers of assault with a deadly weapon and excessive use of force.

The verdict was read at 3:15 p.m. on April 29, 1992, and it shook Los Angeles like an earthquake. Two hours later, the police were called to the intersection of Florence Boulevard and Normandie Avenue in the mostly black neighborhood of South Central Los Angeles, where angry protesters were disrupting traffic and throwing objects at passing cars. A news helicopter's cameras rolled as rioters pulled white truck driver Reginald Denny from his vehicle and, in a grim coda to the King incident, beat him senseless with a fire extinguisher and a brick. By nightfall, the situation in South Central was a full-scale riot and spreading to nearby African-American neighborhoods.

Long-standing tensions between L.A.'s black and Korean-American communities boiled over that night, with hundreds of Korean-owned businesses being burned and looted. Some store owners defended their American dreams with shotguns. Los Angeles mayor Tom Bradley declared a state of emergency. California governor Pete Wilson called in the National Guard. Ultimately, 4,000 U.S. Marines and Army troops were sent in to pacify and patrol the riot-wracked neighborhoods. As the violence escalated, King—who had become, in the words of CNN anchor Bernard Shaw, "the unwilling symbol of this outbreak of violence"— issued an appeal for calm that would instantly become a catchphrase and cultural touchstone. "Can we all get along?" King asked, his voice quavering with emotion. "We've got to quit. After all, I can understand the upset for the first few hours after the verdict, but to keep going on like this...It's just not right."

The Rodney King riots roiled L.A. for three days and caused $1 billion worth of damage to properties and businesses. Fifty-five people were killed and 2,000 people were injured. Most significant, the riots forced the nation to confront the fact that while relations between the police and the black community had cooled since the Civil Rights era, they hadn't actually improved much. It was a cold dose of reality, especially for white members of Generation X, who had for the most part grown up believing the baby boomers' claims that the hard work of racial healing in America had already been done. That's what the hoses and dogs in Selma had been about. That's what the marches and the freedom rides had supposedly accomplished. The L.A. riots showed that racial animus still plagued the country, in part because certain boomer politicians realized they could make great careers for themselves by stoking it.

There were more cold doses of racial reality to come. O. J. Simpson was one of the most recognizable African-American celebrities of the 1970s and '80s, but his appeal transcended race. Like Cosby, Simpson had a crossover personality—he had charisma to burn. In 1968, Simpson won college football's top honor, the Heisman Trophy, at the University of Southern California before proceeding to an 11-year Hall of Fame career as a running back with the Buffalo Bills of the National Football League. His movie-star physique and megawatt smile translated well on the small and large screens. As a television pitchman, he sprinted through airports on behalf of Hertz rental cars. He snagged decent-sized roles in films ranging from serious dramas like Alex Haley's *Roots*, thrillers like *The Raging Inferno*, and comedies like HBO's *1st & Ten*. He was particularly charming—and best known to Generation X—as Officer Nordberg, Leslie Nielsen's accident-prone partner in the *Naked Gun* comedy series, the third installment of which was released in March 1994.

The murders of O. J. Simpson's beautiful, blond ex-wife and a handsome young waiter in a quiet corner of Los Angeles' tony Brentwood neighborhood in June 1994 shocked the world. Popular opinion quickly coalesced around a motive—it was a rage killing by a jealous ex-husband who stalked his former lover during an impromptu rendezvous with a paramour. (History has largely borne this theory out, with the notable exception that Nicole Simpson and Ron Goldman weren't actually lovers). Cops arrested Simpson at his own Brentwood home, kicking off a two-year media spectacle that would provide a template for the let's-see-what-happens-next culture then making its first bold claims on the American imagination. The nation watched Simpson's pre-trial flight in a white Bronco along L.A. freeways with macabre anticipation that the handsome and athletic star would actually commit suicide on live television. As Simpson's friend and chauffeur Al "A.C." Cowlings led LAPD cops on a slow-speed chase through the city, frenzied Angelenos crowded onto overpasses and into intersections with signs urging the duo along.

Simpson's trial was in some ways the first example of the "reality television" that would dominate the airwaves a decade later—always on, frequently salacious, strangely compelling, and unnaturally addictive. The cast of characters was as diverse, flawed, and absorbing as America itself. The plot produced villains and clowns, hints of romantic intrigue, allegations of incompetence, ugly displays of racism, macho posturing, feigned ignorance, procedural legalities, and occasional outbursts of riveting courtroom drama. It was truly what they said it was: the trial of the century.

The not-guilty verdict again laid bare for Generation X the distance between perception and reality of American race relations in the post–Civil Rights era. White Americans saw Simpson's acquittal as a travesty of justice. His high-powered attorneys had obviously manipulated the evidence and the jury to effect an outcome so patently outrageous that all you could do was drop your jaw and gape at it. Black America, on the other hand, saw in Simpson's acquittal a rare and unexpected triumph over a justice system that routinely and unfairly tilts against African-American men. Who was right and who was wrong? Well, it depended on your biases. Your preconceptions about race, crime, and punishment were a good indicator of where you came down on the question of Simpson's guilt or innocence.

It was a bitter lesson for Generation X, and one that would have a greater degree of cultural salience in coming decades, as relativistic theories about class, race, gender, and privilege moved slowly from the most radical corners of academia into the mainstream. For better or worse, Generation X would retain a healthy skepticism of such theories. The generation to come, however, would gobble them up—hook, line, and sinker.

The Simpson trial wasn't the only cultural and political earthquake of the 1990s to shake Generation X's foundational ideas about right and wrong, good and evil, truth and fiction. During the 1980s, politics seemed to most young people like an old man's game. President Reagan was almost 80 years old. His successor, George H. W. Bush, was no spring chicken, either. Even the young guys—such as Dan Quayle and Al Gore—walked and talked like old guys. There wasn't much for Generation X to hang our hats on.

Then, suddenly, there was.

Bill Clinton was the first president many Gen Xers voted for. I turned 18 in 1991, just as what has come to be known as the First Gulf War was ramping up. Iraq's savage dictator Saddam Hussein had invaded Kuwait in August 1990, and throughout the autumn of that year an American military buildup in Saudi Arabia (dubbed Desert Shield) telegraphed that a big and powerful punch (dubbed Desert Storm) was preparing to reverse Saddam's aggression. "This will not stand," declared President Bush, a politician who had up until that very moment suffered from a public perception of weakness. I'm being coy: they called him a wimp.

I and many of my fellow high school seniors had little regard then for the president now frequently called Bush 41. I bought the media portrayal of him as an out-of-touch and slightly dopey puppet on the hand of big business—particularly the oil and gas companies in his home base of Texas. I was young, and youth rarely sees much use in either the oil and gas business or the philosophy of genteel, country-club conservatism that Bush 41 represented, or, rather, that we thought he represented. More immediate to my concerns: Bush 41 seemed like he might try to draft me into the Army and send me to the desert to fight. I was voting for the Democrat, no matter whom it turned out to be.

As it happened, the Democrat turned out to be a fun-loving and youngish-seeming Southern boy with a chubby face and an intellectual bent. Former Arkansas governor Bill Clinton made his mark among people of my generation by going on late night TV and not making a complete fool of himself. He was a political natural, a born communicator. He had a drawl, but he'd been to Oxford. He could talk—boy could he talk. As my Irish grandmother might say, he could talk the hind leg off the Lamb of God. He played the saxophone, if poorly, and seemed genuinely smart and down-to-earth. Nobody doubted that Bush 41 had a certain kind of smarts, but there were very few people in my social circle who considered him down-to-earth. And, there was that famous photo of Clinton as a baby-faced teenager shaking President John F. Kennedy's hand. It was no contest.

During the early months of the 1992 Democratic primary campaign for president, allegations of marital infidelity, as they were then quaintly called, hounded candidate Clinton. When former Arkansas TV reporter Gennifer Flowers told the media that she had had a 12-year affair with Clinton while he was governor of Arkansas, he was forced to deny it. When she played secretly recorded tapes of their conversations at a press conference, Clinton and his wife, Hillary, were forced to give a make-or-break interview to Steve Kroft of CBS's *60 Minutes* in which they both denied that their marriage was a politically convenient mirage.

"You're looking at two people who love each other," Bill said. "This is not some arrangement or understanding."

While acknowledging that he had "caused pain" in his marriage, he flatly denied Flowers's allegations of an affair, claiming that her motivation was purely financial. "It's only when the money came out, when the tabloid went down there offering people money to say they'd been involved with me, that she changed her story," he said. "There's a recession on." Hillary chimed in with a casual smear. Flowers, she said, would call Bill all the time and say "wacky things." Then she delivered the coup de grâce, the line that would rescue her husband's candidacy and, some say, doom her own eventual runs for the White House: "You know, I'm not sitting here some little woman standing by my man like Tammy Wynette. I'm sitting here because I love him and I respect him, and I honor what he's been through and what we've been through together. And you know if that's not enough for people, then heck, don't vote for him."

It was enough. Clinton won the presidency by capturing 370 Electoral College votes with 43 percent of the popular vote. President Bush, the fruits of his desert victory against Saddam Hussein turned rotten by the "it's the economy, stupid" recession, garnered just 37 percent of the popular vote. A great many Americans were unimpressed with either candidate, including my own father, a reliable Democratic voter who cast his lot that year with Ross Perot. The eccentric billionaire won no states but managed to pull down almost 19 percent of the popular vote in one of the most impressive independent presidential bids in American history.

The allegations of sexual impropriety against Clinton didn't go away when he became president. His own political team dismissively referred to them as "bimbo eruptions" and, if anything, they intensified once he moved into the White House. In 1994, former Arkansas state employee Paula Jones filed a sexual harassment lawsuit against the 42nd president. The suit alleged that, in 1991, an Arkansas state policeman lured Jones to a suite in a Little Rock hotel occupied by Clinton, who proceeded to make "abhorrent sexual advances," including dropping his pants and asking Jones to perform oral sex on him. Clinton sought to have the case delayed until the conclusion of his presidency, but an appeals court ruled that the trial should go ahead—a decision that the Supreme Court ultimately affirmed.

Clinton eventually settled with Jones for $850,000, but not before the entire affair and the investigation it spawned nearly brought down his administration. According to the *Washington Post*, the Jones case "opened a Pandora's box of allegations" about Clinton's sex life, including that he had engaged in an 18-month sexual relationship with a 23-year-old former White House intern named Monica Lewinsky. What began life as a sideshow in the Jones case became the main event when special prosecutor Kenneth Starr alleged that Clinton had perjured himself during sworn testimony and urged Lewinsky to lie under oath about the existence of their affair.

As news of the scandal leaked, Clinton wagged his finger at the media and, with a scowl, declared: "I want you to listen to me. I did not have sexual relations with that woman, Miss Lewinsky. I never told a single person to lie, not a single time, never." When the cable networks aired a videotape of his testimony, in which he responded to an interrogator's question with a still-inscrutable reply—"It depends on what your definition of 'is' is"—Americans started to get the hint that maybe the president wasn't telling them the truth, the whole truth, and nothing but the truth about his relations with "that woman, Miss Lewinsky."

Starr's bombshell report to the House of Representatives recommended charging Clinton with 11 articles of impeachment. On December 19, 1998, the House voted for just the second time in American history to impeach the president. Clinton's trial in the Senate on two charges of perjury and obstruction of justice began on January 8 and ended on February 12, 1999. He was acquitted on all counts. Clinton finished out his second term in office, but the effect of the impeachment drama—especially on the twentysomethings of Generation X—was profound and would have a lasting consequence.

The final act of the Bill Clinton presidency was viewed by some as an American tragedy. They read it as a story of a good man laid low by his demons. But the real tragedy was the effect that his public indiscretions had on an entire generation of Americans who forevermore found it nearly impossible to put their full faith and confidence in politicians, no matter their political leanings or party affiliation. Where politics was concerned, the bloom was off the rose for Generation X.

The Clinton years, which had begun with such bright promise on late-night TV in 1992, had ended in the gutter. As the Lewinsky scandal heated up in August 1998, the desperate president lobbed cruise missiles at what he claimed was an Osama bin Laden–owned chemical weapons factory in Sudan, an action viewed by many as an attempt to make him look strong and presidential during the weakest moment of his tenure. The Y2K mini-panic about the possibility of an economy-wide information-technology failure caused by the supposed inability of computers to recognize that the year 2000 was not the year 1900 turned out to be so much hype. On his way out the door, Clinton used his pardon power to offer clemency to Puerto Rican terrorists who had bombed Chicago and New York—killing American citizens—in a bid to secure the support of Gotham's large Puerto Rican population for Hillary's bid to represent the Empire State, where she and Bill had never lived, in the U.S. Senate.

On the final day of his presidency, Clinton also pardoned Marc Rich, a billionaire commodity trader and fugitive from American justice who fled to Switzerland in 1983 rather than face 65 federal criminal counts of tax evasion, wire fraud, racketeering, and, perhaps most sickening of all, flouting the oil embargo on Iran during the time of the hostage crisis. Rich was on the FBI's Ten Most Wanted list and, over the years, had foiled several attempts by U.S. Marshals to return him to the U.S. to face the charges. As the Clinton presidency wound down, Rich had his ex-wife, Denise, a successful songwriter, make a variety of political donations that greased the wheels for a pardon. "In all, Denise Rich made at least $1.1 million in contributions to Democratic causes, including $70,000 to Hillary's Senate campaign and PACs, and at least $450,000 to the Clinton Foundation," according to *CounterPunch* editor Jeffrey St. Clair.

Almost everything Bill Clinton asked the country to believe about his character, his personal life, and his political motivations had essentially been a lie: he *had* cheated on his wife; their marriage *was* an arrangement; he *had* had sexual relations with Monica Lewinsky; he *had* asked Lewinsky to lie under oath. Moreover, there was nothing approaching a "vast right-wing conspiracy" to bring him down, as Hillary Clinton had theatrically alleged in a last-gasp January 1998 interview with Matt Lauer. The Lauer appearance was intended to save Bill's bacon, just as Hillary's Tammy Wynette claims had done six years earlier. It worked, but only barely.

The Clintons had enemies, no doubt about it, but many of them were Democrats and many had sound reason to object to their "co-presidency." There was no conspiracy in the true sense of the word. Rather, it was the man—Bill Clinton—who did this to himself. He brought scandal upon his own presidency through his actions and his ham-handed attempts to cover them up. Every politician has enemies. The savviest take care not to hand their adversaries a hangman's noose.

Taken together, the Rodney King riots, the O. J. Simpson trial, and the Bill Clinton presidency cured Generation X of any lingering idealism that may have been haunting its collective personality following the fall of the Berlin Wall and America's Cold War triumph. In the span of a few years, while Gen Xers were in their late teens to mid-twenties, confidence slipped away that people in positions of influence and authority would do the right thing *because* it was the right thing. We were forced finally to cast a cold eye on the racial and cultural legacy that the baby boomers insisted they were leaving for us. To see an American city that had been in the hands of the supposedly progressive Democratic Party for 30 years erupt into a chaotic insurgency was something we had not been prepared to expect or equipped to handle.

Many cheered the Simpson verdict not because it represented court-room justice. It didn't. They cheered Simpson's acquittal because it represented what they viewed as social justice—a political term of deception that, over the course of the next few decades, would expand to include a host of left-wing social goals and progressive pieties. Social justice, in this view, required a negation of traditional justice. Simpson's acquittal was an overdue smack in the mouth for a system that probably deserved an even more severe rebuke for its habitual mistreatment of minorities. Social justice would do for America what the baby boomers in their excesses of peace, love, and sexual liberation had failed to: create a permanent utopia in which the forces of good would always have dominion over the forces of evil because the forces of good exercised control over the uses of language. If letting O. J. go free was justice, then the word had no meaning. Any horror could be substituted in its place.

Many people defended Clinton's actions as being irrelevant to his ability to perform the job he was elected to do. The economy was blazing, they said. The country was at peace. Everything was more or less just fine during the 1990s. All of this is true to an extent, but there's no denying that the 1990s had a sobering effect on Generation X. The Lewinsky scandal, especially, poisoned the political well for many.

"With polls indicating greater support for Clinton after his affair was made public and Simpson's acquittal despite damning evidence against him, it seemed moral bankruptcy was no longer a symbolic skeleton in the closet to be ousted," wrote Australian scholar Christina Lee in a 2010 examination of cinematic representations of Generation X. "Rather, it was to be expected. The distinction between right and wrong had become relative, easily swayed by the convincing words of a high-priced team of attorneys."

The events I've chosen to highlight here are obviously to some degree subjective. Some loved Bill Clinton then, and love him today. A fair number of people remain convinced that O.J. was framed. Any reasonable person could argue that important and formative events have been left out of this pocket history of Gen X's early years. The signing of the North American Free Trade Agreement, for instance, may have just as much or more to do with our current political predicament than the Rodney King riots ever did. Same with the massacre at Columbine High School.

Gen X isn't a monolith. We don't have homogeneous tastes in music, movies, books, television, or fashion. There are those for whom the deaths of River Phoenix and Kurt Cobain meant a great deal, while the deaths of Tupac Shakur and Biggie Smalls meant next to nothing; and vice versa. Some say their lives were changed when they read what many critics call the sacred text of Generation X, David Foster Wallace's *Infinite Jest*. Others read and hated it. This may be the first time you're hearing about it. Who knows?

I do know that the 1990s revealed to Gen X that something deep and essential about politics, crime, punishment, and justice was a mirage. If the fall of the Berlin Wall gave us the silly idea that the good guys always win, the combined lesson of the Rodney King riots, the O. J. trial, and the Clinton impeachment was that the world isn't perfect and politics can't make it so. Sometimes nobody wins. Often everybody loses. Politics frequently comes down to softening the blow, or deflecting it onto someone else. The knowledge of this didn't turn us into apathetic drips. Nor did it send us crying to the corner with a blankie and a soft pillow. We've managed to do the adult thing, which is to put our heads down and get on with life. Something about our knee-scraped childhoods and the disenchanting sequence of events that colored our early adulthood embedded in us the notion that things will be okay if we somehow summon the fortitude to keep moving forward.

We are a melancholic generation, no doubt about it. We listened to nihilistic grunge, heavy metal, and gangsta rap. The biggest movie of the '90s was *Titanic*, a love story in which most of the characters meet their demise in the icy North Atlantic. Perhaps that sense of melancholy has equipped us with the grit necessary to survive—even to thrive—during periods of terrific social and political upheaval. Maybe it was all the times we heard that old saying repeated by parents, coaches, and gym teachers: life is tough, so get a helmet.

THREE

The End of the Innocence

As the new millennium dawned, Generation X was in flux. Late in the Clinton presidency, the so-called "dot-com" bubble had burst, leveling the life savings of many Xers' parents and throwing the brakes on what had been nearly a decade of vigorous economic growth. The NASDAQ composite index, comprised mainly of information technology stocks, lost nearly 80 percent of its value between 2000 and 2002. Jobs and opportunities across every sector of the economy, previously various and plentiful, began drying up and disappearing. According to the U.S. Department of Labor, the country lost 2.2 million jobs in 2001–02. For Generation X, in our twenties and early thirties, the slowdown couldn't have come at a worse time. We were still paying our student loans, and still trying to get a handle on the adult world of work, savings, family, and the future. It was still the economy, stupid. Maybe it was always going to be the stupid economy that would rule Gen X's life prospects and happiness. What we didn't know in the Year 2000 was just how different the economy would look in 10 years.

Nobody knew. Nobody ever does.

The presidential election of 2000 was yet another circus. Neither the Republican—former Texas governor George W. Bush—nor the Democrat—Vice President Albert Gore—was declared the winner on election night, as had become traditional in the age of television. Gore, who had called Bush to concede early in the evening, retracted his concession as it became clear that results in the crucial state of Florida were "too close to call." A hotly contested recount in the Sunshine State—where Bush's brother Jeb just happened to be the governor—drew squadrons of lawyers from both political parties. The circus was eventually stopped by the Supreme Court on December 12, 2000, with Bush coming out on top as the 43rd president of the United States.

What followed was a season of discontent. Many younger people refused to believe or accept that Bush, who was widely caricatured as an unintelligent buffoon—and, like his father, a puppet on the hand of big business—was the legitimate occupant of the Oval Office. Protesters at his inauguration in January 2001 chanted "Not my president!" The first nine months of the Bush presidency were a late-night comedian's dream come true. He was savaged six ways to Sunday. Given all that has transpired in the nearly two decades since Bush's first year in office, it's easy to forget that he was called an idiot, caricatured as a monkey, and tarred as a theocrat. He was the object of derision, paranoia, even hatred, until a morning of fire changed everything.

Every member of Generation X has his or her own 9/11 story. Some were gathered around television screens in offices in Atlanta, Boston, Chicago, or Nashville. Others were at home, getting ready for work, or in their cars, listening to the radio on their commute. Many on the West Coast were awakened by early-morning phone calls from friends and loved ones around the country. "Get up," they said, "and turn on the television. We're under attack." A woman I know who had a post-college job working for a water-taxi service in New York City spent the entire day ferrying people across New York Harbor, away from lower Manhattan. My oldest sister was halfway around the world, working for a European nongovernmental organization. It was mid-afternoon. When she saw the towers fall, she excused herself from her desk, went into the stairwell, and wept.

I was in New York City, where I lived at the time, heading to John F. Kennedy Airport for a flight to London with the girl who was soon to be my fiancée and eventually my wife. I had the engagement ring in a shoe in my checked luggage. We never made it onto the plane. We barely had enough time to call our parents before the payphones in the terminal went dead. We watched on an airport restaurant television, surrounded by weeping tourists, flight attendants, and fellow travelers, as the towers we knew so well turned to dust. We shared a taxi back to my Queens apartment with strangers while fighter jets screamed across the unbelievably blue skies. It was the worst day of my life. I hope I never experience another like it.

President Bush was in Florida, speaking to a classroom of school-children. He would shortly take to the skies in Air Force One, on the advice of the Secret Service, and spend most of the day crisscrossing the country in an effort to foil the plans of potential assassins. In hindsight, the decision looked silly—the president should have been visible to the American people during this time of crisis. But in real time, as interviews with those in the presidential entourage eventually made clear, the military and intelligence services were just as confused as the general public about who—or what—the next target would be. It was complete chaos. Nobody knew what was coming next. In the course of a few hours, the famous fog of war had spread across an entire nation. I heard some crazy rumors that morning at JFK. Some of them turned out to be true. Most of them didn't.

We'd all learn later about the heroism of the passengers on the doomed United Airlines Flight 93. Among them was Todd Beamer, a 32-year-old husband and father of two. Beamer had been a jock at Wheaton College, a small Christian liberal arts school in the Chicago suburbs. As a senior, he'd been named captain of the basketball team. Fellow student Lisa Brosious knew Todd from his athletic reputation, but told a girlfriend "sometimes people aren't what you think they are." She was right. Todd and Lisa were married in 1994 and moved to New Jersey, where Todd took a job as a software salesman at Oracle Corporation, the kind of job that Gen X go-getters flocked to during the first flush of the dot-com era. The job required a lot of travel, and on the morning of September 11, 2001, Todd caught an early flight to San Francisco out of Newark Airport. Lisa was five months pregnant.

Todd's flight left on time, but as it was passing over Ohio, four al-Qaeda hijackers stormed the cockpit, slit the throats of the pilot, copilot, and at least one flight attendant, herded the passengers to the rear of the plane, and turned the Boeing 757 around. Their target was the Capitol Building in Washington, D.C. Using their old-school flip phones, Beamer and his fellow passengers got word of the attacks already underway in New York. They quickly pieced together their predicament. Beamer tried to place a credit-card call through one of the phones that were then embedded into the seatbacks in some large planes. He was patched through to Lisa Jefferson, a Verizon Airfone call center supervisor in Oakbrook, Illinois. In measured tones, he told her that the plane he was on had been hijacked. "He stayed calm throughout the entire conversation," Jefferson said later. "He made me doubt the severity of the call."

Only when the plane took a sudden nosedive did Beamer raise his voice: "We're going down!"

That nosedive wasn't the end for Flight 93, but the frightened passengers knew they didn't have long to live. They understood that if they let the hijackers carry out their plan, hundreds—possibly thousands—of Americans could die. Beamer, along with rugby player Mark Bingham, judo champion Jeremy Glick, and likely many—if not all—of the others decided to storm the cockpit and, if necessary, fly the plane into the ground. "The hijackers could not have picked a worse plane to hijack than this one," said Jeré Longman, a *New York Times* reporter and author of a book about Flight 93. Nearly every passenger on the plane was, in Longman's words, a "type-A individual."

Beamer told Ms. Jefferson what was about to happen, and the two devout Christians prayed together the famous Psalm 23: "Yea, though I walk through the valley of the shadow of death, I will fear no evil: for thou art with me." Todd left the phone line open as he and his fellow passengers prepared for the final heroic moments of their lives. "Let's roll," Ms. Jefferson heard Todd say, rallying the others for the grim task at hand. She heard the sounds of fighting and commotion. Then—nothing.

No one knows for sure if Beamer and the passengers succeeded in breaching the cockpit door. Longman says that, based on what can be heard on the tape made by the plane's cockpit voice recorder, government investigators believe that they did overpower the hijackers, but it was too late to keep the plane in the air. Flight 93 crashed into a field near Shanksville, Pennsylvania, killing everyone on board. When it hit the ground, the plane was traveling at 575 miles per hour, faster than the planes that hit the World Trade Center. Thirty-seven passengers and seven brave crewmembers lost their lives that morning. Some have called their efforts to retake the plane the first victory in the war on terror.

Beamer and his fellow passengers, like the passengers on the other planes and the people who went to work in the World Trade Center buildings and the Pentagon that cloudless Tuesday morning, found themselves, quite unexpectedly, at the center of a world historical moment. Nearly 3,000 people died on 9/11. More Americans were killed that day than in the Japanese attack on Pearl Harbor in 1941. It was a day that no one who lived through it would, or could, ever forget.

It seems trite now to say that 9/11 was a trauma that caught Generation X by surprise; of course, it caught everyone by surprise, save for a few farsighted American intelligence officials whose warnings went unheeded and the sick individuals who planned the slaughter and carried it out. The global political and military forces that the attacks unleashed, however, came as a particular shock to a generation of Americans who were then still young enough to have the bulk of their lives ahead of them yet old enough to understand that the world they thought they would inherit was likely gone forever. What followed from 9/11 was a decade and a half of war, economic recession, hyper-partisanship, polarization, and a painful—possibly permanent—rending of the social fabric that once held us all together as Americans. In short, not at all the future that the teenagers who had once delighted in the hopeful promise of the end of history and a *Pax Americana* had expected.

Generation X's formative years stretched from the bicentennial jubilee year of 1976 to the national trauma of September 11, 2001. They encompassed the fall of communism and the global wave of democratic hope that it unleashed, as well as the domestic disappointments of the Clinton presidency and the political cynicism that it bred. In 25 years, the nation had gone from behaving like a wounded puppy on the international stage to flexing its considerable muscle as the "indispensable nation," as Secretary of State Madeleine Albright memorably put it. Now, as dawn broke on September 12, 2001, Americans knew that they would soon embark upon a necessary new war, a long war, a costly war waged in some cases against an idea rather than an identifiable foe.

At home, the social and political landscapes had shifted in perceptible and imperceptible ways. A bubble in the American housing market was forming that, when it burst, would nearly collapse the world's financial economy like a grocery-store pyramid of lumpy, rotten apples. President George W. Bush, so recently the object of ridicule, gained a sudden legitimacy. His was now a war presidency. It had a defining mission and so commanded a modicum of respect even from its most fervent critics. Americans did not yet realize that the Bush administration would ultimately sacrifice much of its legitimacy by expanding the war on suspect grounds to target a nation—Iraq—that had nothing to do with the planning and execution of the 9/11 attacks. All of that was still to be revealed.

We weren't there yet, but we'd soon know what it felt like to be constantly tethered to our smartphones and devices, to always be reachable, even on nights, weekends, and holidays. We were beginning to appreciate the benefits of disintermediation of many aspects of the media culture; we'd yet to understand fully the potential costs. The analog age was coming to a close. The digital age was looming.

FOUR

Hard Habit to Break

Among the worst of the baby boomers' social crimes has been their flaccid acquiescence to the still-incoming wowy-zowy technological utopia dominated by Internet connectivity and artificial intelligence, in the process putting untold numbers of artists, businesses, trades, and traditions on the road to extinction. This betrayal is at the heart of the economic and cultural riddle that Gen Xers will have to help unwind. Baby boomers presided over the annihilation of the book store, the record store, and the attention span. They put Starbucks on every corner and Walmarts in every town. They pushed us all out of shop class, gave us laptops and smartphones, and told us that to understand the future we should study computers rather than history, philosophy, or economics. Those who complained were told, "Get with the program. You can't stop progress."

I'm 44 years old. On a typical Saturday morning, I wake up when my 5-year-old toddles into the bedroom I share with my wife and whispers into my ear: "C'mon, Daddy. It's time to get up." Barely conscious, I follow her downstairs and get things ready to make pancakes—a Saturday tradition in our house. I have five children in all. The rest come downstairs according to their sleep schedules and appetites, with the 14-year-old the last to appear.

I would rather die than give up this weekend ritual. Most weekday mornings are a blur. I commute by train into New York City, so I'm always eating breakfast on a deadline. I need to get my lunch made and get myself showered, dressed, fed, and out of the house by 7:30, or the train will leave without me. Breakfast on these days is catch-as-catch-can. Cereal and milk are poured into shallow bowls with careless abandon. Fruit is served in its original packaging. Nothing gets measured, peeled, primped, or plated; everything gets inhaled. It's man, woman, and child for themselves—not what you would call an intimate affair.

Saturday pancakes are a different story. We take our time. We do it right, family style. It's the kids' chance to really pig out on stacks and stacks of Daddy's homemade, maple syrup–smothered flapjacks. It's my chance to chat with my kids, to bond with them, to hoist one or two little bodies up on a stool and let them stir the batter, which I make myself from a recipe handed down from my wife's grandmother. We use real maple syrup, not that imitation corn syrup stuff. The good syrup is much more expensive, and I don't always feel great when I'm shelling out $15–20 for a 16-ounce bottle of it. The other stuff in the lady-shaped bottle costs $4 or thereabouts. But the difference between the real syrup and the corn brew is more than just the price. The authentic syrup costs more because it comes from an actual maple tree planted and tended to for years by real people in Canada or New England. Unlike the fake syrup, which is cooked up according to some proprietary chemical formula and probably tested on lab rats, real maple syrup is harvested by humans using updated and refined versions of traditional methods. Often, these are small farmers—or part-timers—who contribute their annual syrup yield to a local collective or co-op wholesaler.

I cherish my Saturday mornings because I know that one day in the not-too-distant future I'll ask my kids if they'd like me to make them pancakes and they'll say, "Naw, dad. I'm late for class." Or, "Dad, gross, that's too many carbs." I don't know exactly what I'll do when that day comes, but I know it will be a somber occasion. From the first moment I laid eyes on my oldest daughter, I knew that the window was opening on a chapter of life that would not last long. How much time do you get with a child? Eighteen years sounds like an eternity, but it really isn't. Life has a way of speeding up on you as you get older. As some say about parenting, the days are long but the years are short.

The pancakes aren't really the issue. Neither is the maple syrup. They are just set dressing for these special mornings. The kids want pancakes; I want to spend time with the kids.

So why am I always looking at my phone?

Before I get the eggs out of the fridge, brew the coffee, measure flour into the bowl, or heat up the griddle, I reach for my smartphone. Before I even turn on the lights sometimes I'm unplugging my phone and checking my overnight e-mails. Like a lab rat going for his corn-syrup lick, I can't do anything until I satisfy that craving. Usually there's nothing there to check—just the inbox detritus of the Google alerts I've set up, a few podcast downloads, political newsletters I've subscribed to but don't have time to read, sometimes a push alert having to do with breaking news that I'm going to find out about anyway, a sports score. Occasionally an important personal or work e-mail sneaks in, but only occasionally. Most of the time it's absolute junk. Crap-o-la. I check it anyway, obsessively, like a junkie looking for that first fix of the day. I have to have it. I need a taste.

I know it's wrong. I know it's crazy. I know it's totally unnecessary. In fact, I know there's nothing really going on out there that I need to know about at precisely this moment. I mean—*I really do know that.* Yet I can't help myself. I have to find the phone. I have to check Twitter. I have to see if anyone followed me. I have to see if anyone retweeted the story I wrote yesterday. Do I have any friend requests on Facebook? Instagram? Invitations to connect on LinkedIn? I have to see if a highly remunerative job offer came in totally out of the blue.

It's entirely correct to call this behavior pathological. It's irrational and it has an unyielding hold over me. Even as I'm scrolling through the messages and replies, I'm thinking "Why are you doing this?" What compels me—father of five children, lover of small-batch maple syrup, defender of the old ways—to hunt around for my phone every few minutes simply to check whether anyone has pinged me? It's the weekend. It's Daddy Day. I'm not getting paid for this.

I'm in early middle age, still closer to 40 than 50. The impulses that I feel constantly to log in to e-mail, to scan the headlines, to learn the latest—all of that is new. It's a recent development. Very recent. I never used to be this way. I spent hours as a teenager and young adult looking at baseball cards and hockey stickers, flipping through newspapers and old magazines that filled baskets in odd corners of the house, examining and experimenting with the tools on my father's workbench, playing Dungeons & Dragons with my neighborhood friends, Wiffle ball and basketball with my little brother, or noodling around on the cheap guitar that I never quite mastered. I memorized entire scenes from movies. I wrote longhand journal entries in a notebook. Jotted down ideas, poems, sketches, and song lyrics. Never once did I feel the uncontrollable urge to run to the mailbox to see if anything special and addressed to me had been unexpectedly delivered. Sure, I sometimes waited eagerly for the phone to ring. Everyone did in those days. But the phone rang or it didn't. I was expecting a call or I wasn't. I didn't repeatedly pick it up to check if someone was trying to get through. The Internet has trained me to do all that, and it did so in just the past few years.

The technological changes that I've witnessed in my short lifetime have been revolutionary in scope and scale. I was born, raised, and have lived most of my life so far using the same basic analog communications technology that Franklin Roosevelt did: the telephone, the radio, the pen, the postcard, the phonograph record. Sure, Gen Xers had television. FDR didn't have that. But television has always been a one-way street. It's for entertainment, not for communication, and, at least until recently, it was linear, time-limited. You made an appointment to watch television. The show you were looking for was on at a specific hour. You couldn't take it with you. You couldn't dip in and out. If you missed it, well, you missed it. You could check your local listings to see if it would be replayed, but otherwise you were flat out of luck.

Television was even in those days much maligned. No one has ever said that watching a lot of television is good for you. But knowing what we know now, you have to admit: in its own way, television required a certain amount of discipline.

Devices such as the telephone and television—what I call "analog" tools, to distinguish them from the "digital" tools that we are enslaved by today—cultivated patience. Is that possible? We were told back then that television was destroying us, ruining our ability to sustain concentration by presenting shows in attention-span-crushing 30-minute blocks. What would you give to be able to concentrate for 30 straight minutes on a single thing today?

Perhaps we needed some distance to appreciate it, but the telephone and the television *did* reinforce the benefits of patience. It was their prime virtue apart from keeping us entertained, informed, and connected. You wanted to see what happened to Scully and Mulder in the next episode of *The X-Files*, so you put it on your calendar and turned on the TV at the appointed time. Someone said they would call at 7:30, so you cleared a block of time to chat with them at 7:30. You sent someone a letter; you waited for a reply. Sometimes you waited a long time—a really long time. Like children opting to forgo a single marshmallow now for two marshmallows later, we knew that the waiting was good for you. Good things come to those who wait.

The constant waiting cultivated in young people an inherent understanding that media consumption was in some sense a reward for a day spent productively. You got your homework done before *The Cosby Show* came on. You called your friends when the dishes were put away. You went down in the basement and sat on the rug and listened to your records after you cut the grass. Work first; then play. This, then the other.

Of course, not everyone did it this way. In some homes the television was on all day. In some homes there was no television. But, in the main, the technology that was both available and widespread was treated as a tool. You used it. It didn't use you.

Nowadays, with the Internet in our pockets, the concept of media consumption as a bit of recreation after the business of the day is done is as dated as the TV shows I namechecked in the previous paragraphs. For many of us, media—by which I mean use of any device with a screen— is the oxygen we breathe. We need it everywhere. We can't work, play, or relax without it. Actually, it turns out that after two decades of the Internet and a decade of smartphones, we can't even think without it.

As a 2011 *Science Magazine* report noted, our relationship with our technological gizmos and gadgets has changed the way we recall facts and events. Some have dubbed this "the Google effect," after the Internet search engine with the combined market dominance and cultural power of U.S. Steel, Standard Oil, and Ma Bell. Psychologists from Columbia, Harvard, and the University of Wisconsin reviewed four studies that tested how well or poorly people were able to recall information when they knew that a computer would be available to help them save or access that information. On the whole, the test subjects had a harder time recalling details when they knew that those details had been stored on a computer and that they could access them again when they needed to. In fact, they often had an easier time remembering where on the computer the information had been stored than they did remembering the information itself.

"Because search engines are continually available to us, we may often be in a state of not feeling we need to encode the information internally," the authors of the study noted. "When we need it, we will look it up." The reverse is also true. When we know we won't be able to look things up, it's easier for us to remember them. "[I]t appears that believing that one won't have access to the information in the future enhances memory for the information itself . . . [w]hereas believing the information was saved externally enhances memory for the fact that the information could be accessed, at least in general."

In other words, we are treating the Internet as an external brain. Our real brains know they no longer have to work as hard as they once did, so they naturally start slacking off. The social price for this transformation has been high. In a 2016 interview with C-SPAN's Brian Lamb, the historian David McCullough sketched it out: "We've been told we live in the information age. And we get information in quantities such as would have been unimaginable in other times—and on an infinite variety of subjects, and all that can come instantly electronically, and in many ways you don't have to carry any of this in your head," he said. What's the tradeoff? "You can just look it up, so why learn it?"

The idea that you can "just look it up" may seem a boon. The goal of a good education, after all, isn't to fill your head with facts (although that is often a happy byproduct of a good education). Rather, someone who has been well educated knows enough to know what he doesn't know. The problem now is that an entire generation of kids have grown up, graduated from high school and college, and are working their way through the professional world without knowing what they don't know . . . *because they don't know anything*. The ethos they have imbibed is, in fact, not to know. Knowledge is outsourceable. Google is standing at the ready, waiting to help them anytime they're ready to "just look it up." These are the so-called "digital natives," born into an end-of-century wilderness just as it was wiring itself up for the leap to technological hyperspace. We call them millennials.

The "just look it up" millennial mindset has contributed in large measure to the dumbing down of the culture. A 2015 survey of college professors and employers commissioned by the education reform group

Achieve found that while American high schools do a decent job of preparing students to use technology and collaborate in teams, they do a far worse job of preparing them to write in plain English, think complex problems through, and understand complicated written materials or ideas. A vanishingly small percentage of professors and employers said they thought that American high school graduates were ready to "do what was expected of them." Why? Is it because high school teachers are worse today than they were 70 years ago? No; it's because most kids don't have the ability or desire to concentrate longer than it takes to read a disappearing Snapchat. Social media and the quick-hit Internet have trained them to click away from anything that doesn't hold their attention for more than the time it takes to yawn.

A 2014 study found that college students spend an enormous amount of time each day using smartphones and the Internet. The females studied spent 10 hours every day online, while the males spent about 7.5 hours online daily. "Research suggests that media use has become such a significant part of student life that it is 'invisible' and students do not necessarily realize their level of dependence on and/or addiction to their cell-phones," wrote researchers in a paper published in the *Journal of Behavioral Addiction*. Other researchers have studied the ability of college students to concentrate on a lecture while being barraged with text messages to which they feel obligated to respond. Those who received 16 or more texts during a 30-minute lecture scored a full letter grade lower on a post-lecture exam than those who received half as many texts. Millennials are driven to distraction by their technological addictions.

It's affecting their grades, their performance on the job, and their ability to be present in personal relationships. But they're so-called "digital natives," born and raised in the Internet era, so they don't even recognize it as a problem. It's just life. Texting is living.

Don't get me wrong—grown-ups these days can't concentrate, either, and my pancake distraction is a prime example. A Canadian study showed that while the average human attention span was 12 seconds in 2000, nearly 20 years of Internet influence has pushed that down to 8 seconds. We are all losing our ability to sustain concentration. We're letting our focus slip, and we've all gone voluntarily down this path. It's a problem if, like me, you're in middle age, but at least a guy like me can search for solutions to the problem with the full knowledge of how things used to be—how much easier it was in the pre-Internet days to settle down with a book without thinking about your phone, or to be alone with yourself (or your family) for a few hours. If you are a high school student in the late second decade of the 21st century—or the parent of such a child—this is not just a problem; it's a crisis. A high school English teacher told me recently that she watches in amazement as her students Google basic facts and information that once formed the mere minimum of what a person should know by the time he or she reached adolescence. Things are going downhill fast.

Neil Postman saw it coming. The author and humanist died in 2003. He lived, worked, and wrote well before the arrival of the iPhone and social media, but as what we call the Internet was emerging wet and flightless from its "information superhighway" chrysalis during the 1990s, he was practically alone in predicting how the headlong rush to embrace it would play out. Many during those early days were sold on the idea that the new era of rapid information search and connectivity would unleash human potential on a scale not seen since the advent of the printing press. The tradeoff in terms of whatever was going to be lost to this new and spectacular technology, they thought, would be worth it.

Postman was not convinced. Here he is in a 1995 interview with PBS's Charlene Hunter Gault:

> I've mostly decided that new technology—[the Internet] or any other kind—is a kind of Faustian bargain. It always gives us something important, but it also takes away something that's important. That's been true of the alphabet, the printing press, telegraphy, right up through to the computer. For instance, when I hear people talk about the "information superhighway"—it will become possible to shop at home, to bank at home, to get your texts at home and get your information at home, and so on—I often wonder if this doesn't signify the end of any meaningful community life. I mean, when two human beings get together and they're co-present, there's built into it a certain responsibility we have for each other. And when people are co-present in family relationships and other relationships, that responsibility is there. You can't just turn off a person. On the Internet, you can. And I wonder if this doesn't diminish the built-in human sense of responsibility we have for each other.

The Internet gives us access to an infinity of information, which back in the pre-Internet era seemed like a good deal. One of the defining characteristics of human history has been asymmetrical access to information. Leveling that playing field promised to be a major civilizational advance. There has been an upside—much of it well-documented. Less well appreciated have been the very significant tradeoffs.

Some of the tradeoffs we can see—people who can't hang out with their kids on a Saturday morning without jonesing for a look at their iPhones. Or worse—people who are crashing their cars into telephone poles because they can't drive 10 minutes to the store without replying to their text messages. But many of the truly damaging tradeoffs don't show up on the evening news. The number of teenagers with attention deficit/hyperactivity disorder skyrocketed 43 percent between 2003 and 2011. Researchers from Kaohsiung Medical University Hospital in Taiwan found a link between ADHD and Internet addiction.

The tech journalist Nicholas Carr charted the devastating effect that the Internet is having on our brains in his indispensable 2010 book *The Shallows*. "The possibility of intellectual decay is inherent in the malleability of our brains," he writes. We know that the brain can reorganize itself. Whether in response to injury or a changing environment, the synaptic connections that govern how we experience and interpret the world are extraordinarily adaptable. Scientists call this "neuroplasticity." It's the product of evolution, and mostly a good thing. We need to rewire our hard drives once in a while. But mental illness, addiction, and a host of unhealthy habits can be imprinted onto our neural pathways through repetition. The brain doesn't develop in only one direction.

"As the many studies of hypertext and multimedia show, our ability to learn can be severely compromised when our brains become overloaded with diverse stimuli online," writes Carr. "More information can mean less knowledge."

More information can mean less knowledge—how can that be? A phenomenon Carr calls "digital overload" can make it hard to "distinguish relevant information from irrelevant information." In order to do that, you need to spend some time in the real world. In order to develop the capacity to distinguish useful information from garbage, you need to have developed the capacity to relate to the world around you—both the social environment and the natural environment. In the pre-Internet era that

Gen X and every previous American generation grew up in, figuring out a method of relating to the world required almost no conscious effort. People developed such personal habits of mind and body organically. In the post-Internet world, suddenly, we find ourselves in the unexpected position of having to coach our millennial cousins—those digital natives—on the importance of maintaining a connection with reality.

FIVE

Smothered in Hugs

The first dollar I ever spent on myself was plunked onto the glass counter at Scotti's Records on South Street in my hometown of Morristown, New Jersey. Actually, it was 10 dollars. The year was 1984. I was 11 years old. More than three decades later, the memory of the purchase I made that day still has the power to make me blush. I was burning to spend the 10-spot I had been given on my 11th birthday on a new record, a hot record, something that I could take home and play as many times as I liked. It had to be a record that I just couldn't live without. So I brought my small fortune to Scotti's and selected from the display rack of Top Ten records my own fresh, shiny copy of Duran Duran's *Seven and the Ragged Tiger*.

I wasn't savvy enough yet to know that Duran Duran was maybe not the kind of band that an 11-year-old boy should broadcast his appreciation for, but you have to understand the context. The British synth-pop pioneers' videos featured Simon Le Bon and John Taylor dressed in rainforest adventure gear, jumping in slow motion through waterfalls and waving torches for "New Moon on Monday." They were stylish and exciting and new—in other words, not the Monkees or Led Zeppelin or Credence Clearwater Revival that an 11-year-old in 1984 heard pouring out of radios in passing muscle cars or at backyard barbecues. It was modern electropop in all its uncomplicated glory, and I was unashamed to enjoy it.[6]

Buying tapes and records in those days was no everyday thing. Walking into Scotti's was, for me, like walking into an exotic Moroccan bazaar. Apart from the limited selection of artists that made it onto radio or MTV—or having teenaged older sisters, which I did—there was no way of knowing what new records had been released or what cool new bands had been bubbling up. Maybe you had a subscription to one of the better music magazines or to *Rolling Stone*, which could tell you a little about what was coming next and what was popular among interesting people with good taste. But when you got to the shop, you simply had to browse, look around, let your fingers do the walking through endless alphabetical bins packed tight with glorious, glistening, shrink-wrapped LPs.

Records were physically large. They looked like something you could hang on the wall. A lot of people did just that. The ones you bought would take their place in a milk crate in your basement alongside the other stuff you loved and listened to. It was your collection. It was a real thing, tangible, fragile, worth protecting—with your life if necessary. Contrast this to the modern iTunes library or Spotify playlist via which millennials discover and listen to music. The person who would fight to protect such things would probably fight over anything.

A record collection, no matter how big or small, said something about who you were. It broadcast your tastes and preferences to everyone who visited your house and took a moment to check out your setup. When you became a teenager and started riding around in cars, your tape collection—housed in the glove compartment, the passenger-side armrest, under the hand brake, in a briefcase under the front seat, or sloshing around on the dashboard—gave passengers something to peruse while you and they cruised without a care on teenage streets. It was your rolling soundtrack, played loud and with the windows rolled down; it said as much about who you were, what you liked (and what you could

---

6 About a year later I would get my cool card punched when I brought $15 down to Scotti's and shelled out for cassette copies of the Smiths' *Strangeways Here We Come* and the Pogues' *Rum, Sodomy, and the Lash*, which, by the time I was through with it, could only be identified by the cover art on the tape box—the printed words on the side of the tape had been worn off by constant play.

afford) as your clothes or your haircut did. Friends made tapes for each other, mixes that prefigured the modern digital playlist, but required time and dedication to assemble. It wasn't click and drag, it was play and record—two buttons, pressed simultaneously, and the smoother the transition between tracks the better. The best mixes were seamless.

Enjoying music before the digital revolution kicked off was not just an auditory affair; it was physical. You had to push fat buttons, find grooves, flip discs, replace needles, lower arms, buff scratches, balance speakers, patch tears, adjust speeds, clean heads, unspool tape with pencils, fiddle knobs, rewind, fast-forward, reverse sides, and apologize for the odd scratch. He who had mastered these dark arts was rewarded with soothing waves of rich stereo sound.

All of that fiddling and faddling went out the window with the advent of the compact disc. That format's auditory offerings were a mile wide and a digital-inch deep. You heard more things but the sound was worse. You couldn't feel the waves of whumping bass, crystal mids, and sparkling treble washing over you the way you had when you sat on the rug in the basement in front of those big, boxy speakers. Once the MP3 arrived on the scene in the late 1990s, it was game over for the touchy-feely audiophile. The physical experience of buying and playing music was dead and buried. With the exception of a community of die-hards and hobbyists, the culture of the 45, the EP, and the LP—of vinyl and tape—has gone the way of the dodo.

Because of many such common experiences in that pre-Internet moment, most Gen Xers share certain similar dispositions regarding the uses and limits of technology. Our outlook was shaped by a childhood defined by slow but steady improvements in the quality of the electronic gear we brought into our homes. We had telephones, first rotary, then push-button. They were attached to the wall. They were immobile appliances—practically furniture. We took calls at the kitchen table, or on the basement stairs, or in the closet. Wherever the twisted, curly cord would stretch long enough to give a teenager some privacy, that's where we could be found, chatting about the important things and plotting out the slowly approaching opening scenes of our adult lives. We were constantly told by adults and older siblings to hang up, to free the line, and, in the exasperated words of the mystified father of one of my friends, to "state your business and get off!"

Before every home had a computer, every home had a typewriter. Some were manual, some electric. All were temperamental. We dragged them up to our rooms to write letters, book reports, college essays, and term papers. Formal business letters required formatting that had to be learned and followed. We changed ribbons and used Wite-Out to correct our typos. There was no delete, no cut-and-paste, no undo or redo or select all, no find-and-replace, no saving of updated versions. You had to do the whole thing by hand. You had to take your time and get it right. It was worth the extra time it took to write out in longhand what you wanted to type before you sat down to wrangle with the strange and indomitable machines. Typing paper and ribbons cost money.

In school we worked on mainframe computers to learn BASIC programming.

```
10 PRINT Matt Is the Best
20 GOTO 10
30 END
```

Eventually we plugged napkin-sized floppy disks into boxy personal computers that did little more than process words and play crude-looking games. A few years after that we got bing-bong-shhhh modems that dialed up to America Online or some other proto-Internet service provider. We slowly learned to check our e-mails. First, once a month; then, once a week; then every other day. We visited libraries when we needed to look things up, or we asked an older person, many of whom, we came to appreciate, knew a lot of things that we didn't know. We used print shops like Kinko's to run off copies of our typewritten resumes. When traveling, we drank coffee in that quintessential '90s establishment—the Internet café. There, we'd catch up on e-mails and write back to our far-flung friends.

Most of us we weren't checking in daily on the Internet until the very late '90s or early 2000s. Some of us, of course, were what we now call "early adopters"—always grabbing the newest and latest gadget or app before everyone else (and discarding it, too, before the general population got the message that it was yesterday's Big Deal). Beepers, answering services, and PalmPilots all had their day. The constant-contact, deep-immersion world of Internet obsession didn't overtake us until we were in our thirties. For Generation X—unlike for those who came after—the constant commotion of the Internet-saturated world snuck up like old age. Unlike the millennials, we know how life was lived before. We remember. If we can manage to hang onto it, that memory of the way things used to be will serve us well in the coming years and decades, as digital technology and artificial intelligence reach ever deeper into the daily rhythms of our lives, distorting everything they touch and turning us all into screen-addicted, inward-facing zombies.

* * *

David McCullough is an old man. Perhaps that gives him the perspective necessary to see the approaching danger more clearly than most. In a speech at Boston College in 2008, the distinguished historian with the all-American voice delivered a prophetic message. Most of that year's graduating class had been born in 1986 and 1987—the hot center of the millennial cohort. They were the first class that had been helped through high school by Google, one of the most useful benchmarks for determining whether you're millennial or Gen X.

These newly minted graduates had searched for a college to attend and applied for admission to it entirely online. They may have snail-mailed in their personal references or financial aid applications, but they'd received their acceptance letters via e-mail. At freshman orientation they exchanged cell-phone numbers and Myspace profile information with their new friends. Facebook was launched during their first year in college and began its rapid march to dominance of campus social interactions before spidering its way into every corner of American life. Although the full impact of Facebook, social media, and the avalanche of what we've come to call fake news was not yet fully in view in 2008, McCullough's remarks were prophetic. Something ominous was coming, and the wise old sage could sense its presence:

> Facts alone are never enough. Facts rarely, if ever, have any soul. In writing or trying to understand history, one may have all manner of data, and miss the point. One can have all the facts and miss the truth. It can be like the old piano teacher's lament to her student, "I hear all the notes, but I hear no music."

The social ecology of the Internet—so full of notes, so devoid of music—has governed the lives of the young Americans we call millennials.

It shaped their childhoods and accompanied them through school. It is their best friend, the one they turn to for counsel, companionship, medical advice, and relationship support. It is where most of them feel most comfortable. They are digital natives, after all. The Internet is their home.

But who are they really? What is a millennial?

The term has been banging around among social scientists for a while, but it's fair to say that it broke through to the wider culture only about 10 years ago. Unlike the term Gen X, a descriptive tag dreamed up after the fact to capture and convey what looked like extended adolescence, or baby boomer, which derives from an actual biological phenomenon, the millennial generation was always on the calendar. The late 1990s were a period of profound confusion about the future. The looming millennium—the mythical Year 2000—was for many 20th-century Americans a symbol of a future too distant to contemplate. A common pastime among people my age was to calculate how old you would be when that millennial bell tolled on the midnight between December 31, 1999, and January 1, 2000. I would be 27. In my youth it sounded to me like a terribly sophisticated and mature age to be, an age at which I would for sure have figured out not only my identity but also my purpose. To a child, 27 may as well be 57 or 87.

The world was bracing itself as the Year 2000 grew nearer, though for what, it didn't know. The late American musical superstar Prince put down a marker in the early 1980s with his party anthem "1999." The subtitle of the first part of Tony Kushner's epic AIDS drama *Angels in America* was titled "Millennium Approaches." In his worldwide 1998 hit "Millennium," the British pop star Robbie Williams crooned, "We've got stars directing our fate and we're praying it's not too late."

Too late? For what exactly?

Something big seemed like it was coming. During the last five years of the 1990s, the endless repetition of ill-defined catchphrases like the "World Wide Web" and "the information superhighway" had many older Americans scratching their heads. What did it all portend? Some said the world's electronic infrastructure would fail in a cascading catastrophe related to the Y2K bug. Some feared the possibility of a terrorist attack aimed at the many large outdoor celebrations planned in cities around the world. In that pre-9/11 world, the 1996 Olympic bombings in Atlanta provided the predicate for such a horror. Motivated by anti-abortion sentiments and a desire to punish the U.S. government by forcing the cancellation of the games, Eric Robert Rudolph set a backpack full of pipe bombs and nails beneath a bench near an outdoor concert on July 27, 1996. The explosion killed one person directly; another died of a heart attack in the aftermath. More than 100 other people were injured by either the shower of shrapnel or the resulting stampede.

A similar attack, or a worse one, on New Year's Eve 1999 seemed a real possibility, one that authorities all over the world were fretting over and trying to prepare for. A few wilder imaginations even entertained the possibility of a true millennial event—a world-ending meteor, a series of continent-destroying volcanic earthquakes, or the second coming of Jesus Christ.

If the approaching millennium surfaced strange anxieties, there was also profound hope in the air. The Soviet menace was gone. The light of freedom and democracy was flooding into once dark corners of the earth. America stood alone as a superpower on the world stage. The great bloody conflagrations of the previous century seemed to be receding. So did intractable smaller conflicts. The Troubles that had bedeviled Northern Ireland for three bloody decades came to an end with the Good Friday Agreement signed in 1998. It was actually beginning to look like the end of history.

Children born during the 1990s were cooed over and cradled by grandparents who had lived through the Great Depression and the liberation of Europe. Those members of the silent and greatest generations carried with them memories of their own parents and grandparents, whose lives stretched back to World War I, the Gilded Age, and beyond. To be a millennial was to be a child passed across the threshold of continuity into a new and potentially unlimited future. "Millennial" is in itself an epic handle. But if the children of the 1980s and '90s were born under an auspicious star, they also had the bad fortune to come along at the same time that a truly cosmic force was gathering: the Internet.

Tim Berners-Lee, the British computer scientist generally credited with inventing the World Wide Web, built the first web browser around 1991, when the oldest millennials were roughly 10 years old. An explosion of intellectual and engineering fervor followed. By 1995, as the leading edge of the millennial cohort was entering its teen years, many of the online brands that would dominate the first decade of the Internet era were making their appearances in the marketplace and their first claims on the American mind: Amazon, Yahoo!, eBay, Microsoft's Internet Explorer web browser. In 1996, America Online began offering a $19.95 monthly dial-up Internet service and carpet-bombing mailboxes with its free-trial CDs. The Internet—which had previously been the plaything of nerds, geeks, gamers, and computer scientists—suddenly became the new consumer "must have." The masses now had easy access to cheap e-mail and web browsing, chat rooms and interactive games. Search was still a problem. Yahoo! was the main search engine in use at the time, but there was a small ecosystem of competitors like Lycos, Infoseek, HotBot, Excite, and the tragically named Ask Jeeves. These sites helped the average person to poke around in this bewildering new environment and its still uninteresting offerings.

Google, which launched in late 1998, opened the whole thing up. Pre-Google, surfing the web was like reaching from tree to tree in a dense forest on a pitch-black night. You wanted to be sure not to stray too far from where you started lest you become disoriented and lose track of the way home. Google was like the sunrise. Suddenly everything that had been shadowy and confusing came into full view. Information you came across online started to make sense. It connected. You could hop from one page to the next in something like a logical order. You no longer had to feel your way.

After 1998 nothing was the same. The Internet and its garden of delights became a daily destination for most people. Only the oldest millennials can recall a time when that limitless horizon of information wasn't a mere mouse click away. If you are a millennial, the Internet has always been standing idly by, waiting to answer your questions, big or small, whatever they may happen to be. As you grew older, it developed the ability to fulfill your real-world requests. Now, in 2018, it can order any consumer good, transfer any fund, shuffle any playlist, pause any movie, or download any book directly to any handheld device. It can anticipate your needs. It can think for you if you need it to, helping you to decide what you want if you don't already know. To the extent that any millennial retains a memory of a time without the Internet, it's an impossibly dim and unreliable one, sort of like how my own father, born in 1935, claims to remember Civil War veterans marching in the local Memorial Day parade when he was young. It's a mental mirage. He remembers them, all right, but only because he knows he's supposed to. His logic tells him they were there, so he draws them into his memories.

Gen Xers will never be fully at home in this digital domain. We didn't grow up with this stuff. We will always be exiles from the analog world. Most of us have acclimated and assimilated to life in the Internet forest, but it remains in our minds a dark, dangerous, mysterious, and new place. We are like immigrants who find a way to live, even to prosper, in a land where we are never quite at ease.

To the millennials, on the other hand, the Internet is their native peat. They are on terra firma there, at ease, relaxed, in their element. The dangers that David McCullough warned of—facts without soul, notes without music—do not appear to this Gen Xer to be something that millennials are overly concerned about. It just is what is, like the air you breathe or the wallpaper in your childhood bedroom. It feels right. It smells like home. Asking a millennial to critique or question the Internet-soaked world is like asking him to disown his hometown and all his friends and relatives. Pointing out the flaws and shortcomings of the wired-up way we live now is like inviting him to commit treason. Questioning its benevolence is like admitting you prefer darkness over light. The millennials are too invested in the Internet to accept the idea of a world without it—or with less of it.

Encouraged by Silicon Valley's string of tangible technological successes, not to mention its utopian promises, few millennials will admit a downside to moving every form of human interaction onto the web or disrupting every established way of doing business. They see no problem transferring their personal information and documents to the so-called cloud, or wiring up every appliance and device into the Internet of Things. They have no anxiety about this new way of living because they have no memory of the old way of living. They see only an upside to the creative destruction of the sharing and gig economies as embodied by companies like Uber and Airbnb. The app-based Internet world is where they want to live. A Silicon Valley superfirm like Google is where they want to work. They look forward to the arrival of the driverless cars that will transport us quickly and with carbon-minimized efficiency between points in the dense, bike-friendly cities where they tell pollsters they'd prefer to make their homes. Technology offers them ease of communication and ease of movement. It offers them an economy they desire—full of free journalism, free music, free movies, and free information. Privacy is meaningless. Nothing is lost. All is upside.

Au contraire; much has been lost. Much more will be sacrificed at the altar of technological "progress" before the transformation envisioned in Silicon Valley breakrooms, Portland sushi restaurants, Austin yoga studios, and Williamsburg coffee shops is complete.

The millennials' first tragic glimpse of the big world on 9/11 convinced them at an impressionable age that unpredictable and untamable forces govern everything. They were for the most part too young to understand the details, but they internalized a larger message: the real world is a chaotic place, where fire and death can rain down in an instant, where serenity is an illusion. Smart people will disagree on the psychological and emotional effects such a public catastrophe has on children, and how those effects might shape those children's development as they grow older. The demographer Neil Howe, who along with William Strauss is credited by many with having coined the term "millennial," has surmised that the intensity of the 9/11 experience and its civic aftermath fostered in millennial children a desire for greater personal and familial intimacy than was sought by preceding generations. Put simply, frightened millennial kids closed ranks with mom and dad, who were themselves deeply shaken by what they had seen that terrible morning.

Parents of millennials naturally sought to shelter their young children from the worst of the fallout from 9/11: the ever-present images of smoking ruins, the litany of the names of the dead, the public displays of raw emotion. Grieving adults spoke in hushed tones about the news of the day so children wouldn't have to hear all the gory details. But the kids picked up on it, as they always do.

"Risk aversion is something that's huge [for millennials]," Howe told *Morning Call* reporter Andrew Wagaman in 2016. "It cuts across so many aspects of their lives—drinking, smoking, finances, you name it." Is this reticence a character trait attributable to the trauma of 9/11? No one can say definitively, but it's a plausible theory. A 2017 study of entrepreneurship posited that millennials start fewer companies than other generations in part because of an inherent fear of taking risks.

The eruption of patriotism and national unity that followed the 9/11 attacks mirrored in a way the national party of the 1976 Bicentennial.

American flags appeared in apartment-house windows and on urban fire escapes as well as on the backs of small-town pickup trucks and national politicians' lapel pins. The sentiment was similar—E Pluribus Unum—but the country had changed in ways too numerous to catalog in the intervening quarter century.

The appetite for free-range parenting, which was the undisputed norm in 1976, had waned considerably by 2001. The millennials' parents had already developed a reputation for "helicoptering"—hovering nearby to provide instant assistance to children who wandered into challenging or potentially dangerous situations. The 9/11 tragedy may have affected parents, children, and communities in similarly unhealthy ways, drawing them closer and closer together in a protective embrace at precisely the wrong time. It had the feeling of intimacy, but the closing of the ranks may have hastened the demise of the nurturing culture of "benign neglect" that was once broadly accepted as the best way to condition children to survive and adapt in a dangerous and unpredictable world.

The invasion of Iraq in 2003 offended the millennial conscience. They were becoming teenagers by then, and equipped with all the capacity for moral outrage for which that particular age range is justifiably famous. Indeed, for the most part the millennials viewed the entire George W. Bush presidency as one long ballet of incompetence: war, mismanagement, natural disaster, political scandal, skyrocketing student debt, and, ultimately, financial collapse. Add to this potent admixture an unprecedented dose of parental indulgence, breakneck technological change, mean-spirited political polarization, and college educations at the hands of post-modern, post-structuralist, post-free-speech campus radicals—and, voila, you get the millennials: the neediest, least adventurous, least self-aware, least historically attuned generation of Americans yet.

I know not all millennials fit the stereotype of the whiny, fragile Snapchat addict. Many prefer paperback books to iPhones. Some would rather work at the same company for 45 years than gig as a freelance Brooklyn jobber bopping from brunch to spin class to the juice bar and back. The upsurge in popularity of local produce, slow food, home brewing, old-fashioned shaving kits, handlebar mustaches, knitting, and other hipster fascinations is indicative of some deep-seated longing for authenticity among millennials that isn't being fully met. Some of it seems ostentatious and phony, but some of it seems sincere and right on the money. A heroically large number of millennials are overseas at this very minute in war zones, hotspots, and refugee camps, sacrificing of themselves and putting their lives on the line for the freedom and security of people they've never met and never will. Some even smoke real cigarettes. No millennial looks in the mirror in the morning and sees his generation.

But, still.

The millennials have taken a reputational beating in the last few years, some of it gratuitous, most of it justified. They are needy nellies who can't take a joke. They are job-hopping know-it-alls who actually know very little. Millennials already constitute more than half the American workforce, and employers have bent over backward to accommodate their habits and preferences. Millennial impatience with traditional business practices is no secret, and the hierarchy-disregarding office millennial has become a familiar cultural type. Their first job was for many millennials the first time anyone asked them to do something boring, monotonous, unenticing, or—that most millennial of insults—basic. Many expect to be promoted during their first year on the job.

"I think the younger generation obviously wants to move a lot more quickly in positions than maybe the more senior folks like me," said Kathleen L. Flanagan, president and CEO of the consulting firm Abt Associates, in a 2013 interview with the *New York Times*. "They're constantly curious about what they can do next. They're almost impatient about sitting in a job for any length of time, and they always wonder about the next opportunity. There's obviously tension there." A nonprofit CEO once told me that a millennial employee had asked him bluntly during a performance review, "What have you got planned for me?"

From whence does this impatience come? The millennials were mollycoddled as children, according to the conventional wisdom. Helicoptering parents governed their social interactions like a Hollywood publicist crafting a respectable career for his stable of clients. Everything was stage-managed. Playdates, birthday parties, athletic events, study groups, teacher relationships, volunteer opportunities, cultural exposure, and family dinners were planned and executed with an eye to creating a friction-free glide-path toward college, career, and relationship success. Millennials rode in car seats until they were 10. They wore bike helmets and knee pads lest they got a boo-boo. They were never allowed out of sight, lest they fell into an open manhole or got abducted by a stranger. They never roamed the neighborhood alone, waited at a bus stop on a freezing dark morning, or were told they weren't good at something even when it was true. They were driven to school and carried all the way to the finish line of high school graduation.

Tutored. Tailored. Never tested. The millennial childhood was free of danger, devoid of risk, and guard-railed from pole to pole by doting parents. At least, that's the stereotype. Is it true? Yes, insomuch as every stereotype carries a grain of truth. Beyond that, all that can be said is what has been said over and over in these pages, and will continue to be said: everyone is an individual, but generational cohorts do tend to share certain observable characteristics. Pretending they don't exist—or don't matter—is just as irresponsible as pretending they explain everything.

In a 2013 *TIME* cover story, journalist Joel Stein called millennials "lazy, entitled narcissists" weaned on participation trophies and excessive self-esteem. He cited a National Institutes of Health study that found millennials three times more likely than baby boomers to suffer from narcissistic personality disorder. "It turns out that self-esteem is great for getting a job or hooking up at a bar but not so great for keeping a job or a relationship," wrote Stein. "All that self-esteem leads them to be disappointed when the world refuses to affirm how great they know they are."

Here's where it gets really dicey. Millennials' high opinion of themselves doesn't extend to the country they share with older generations. Markedly less patriotic than boomers and Gen Xers, they see nothing particularly special about being American and recoil at the notion of American exceptionalism. A 2017 cross-generational study by the research firm 747 Insights found that less than half of millennials consider the United States "the greatest country in the world." By contrast, 63 percent of Gen Xers and 68 percent of boomers see the U.S.A. as being in some fundamental sense a superior place to be born, raised, and to live out your life.

A 2016 Gallup Poll found that socialism was more popular than capitalism among those under 30. Nearly 70 percent of millennial survey respondents said that they'd be comfortable voting for a socialist candidate. During the 2016 Democratic presidential primary, 80 percent of voters under 30 voted for Bernie Sanders in the crucial early-voting states of Iowa, New Hampshire, and Nevada. These attitudes set millennials apart from Generation X and the baby boomers, but it's Generation X that will feel their impact as the double-wide millennial cohort ages and begins its inexorable takeover. The advertising world has already begun to turn away from marketing to middle-aged Xers, catering instead to millennials and their massive purchasing power. Like the baby boomers, the millennial generation dwarfs Gen X.

Even the military is scrambling to adapt to the needs of its youngest recruits. The Army has considered prolonging the amount of time that drill sergeants spend with new soldiers during basic training. "The problem that we do have is that right now the generation we have coming in is not as disciplined as we would like them to be," a spokesman told *Army Times* in 2016. "So we have to provide them with discipline over a longer period of time." One of the concerns with millennial recruits is that some of their generational needs and characteristics are at odds with traditional military culture. Before following an order, for instance, millennials want to know why it was issued. Not exactly the attitude that helps wins wars.

As the millennial wave moves through the economy, every industry could soon resemble Silicon Valley, where recent college graduates consistently rate high-flying information technology and lifestyle firms like Google and Apple as the companies they'd most like to work for. The tech industry's youth obsession has produced some strange outcomes. The *New Republic*'s Noam Scheiber reported in 2014 that "ageism" in Silicon Valley has led executives in their late thirties and early forties to turn to cosmetic surgery in order to extend their careers. The experience and seasoning of these Gen X techies don't count for much within Silicon Valley's youth-obsessed culture: "In the one corner of the American economy defined by its relentless optimism, where the spirit of invention and reinvention reigns supreme, we now have a large and growing class of highly trained, objectively talented, surpassingly ambitious workers who are shunted to the margins…for reasons no one can rationally explain." To an industry selling a better tomorrow, fortysomething Gen Xers like me carry the unmistakable smell of yesterday. That makes us pretty much worthless.

Perhaps most troubling, millennials have displayed an aggressive indifference to the bedrock American principle of free speech. This is a new development. Every generation has had its extreme political movements, and the United States during the 20th century certainly had its fair share. At one time or another, everyone from the Yippies to the Nation of Islam to the Westboro Baptist Church to the Black Israelites managed to push their strange and perverted philosophies into the national debate over the boundaries of political acceptability. Often they did so by inviting confrontation through rallies, speeches, and other public forms of political expression. Inasmuch as everyday Americans were forced to interrupt their daily comings and goings to listen to and regard these groups—in a public park, on a college campus, or on the courthouse steps—they were mostly revolted by what they heard. But the revulsion was tempered by a sometimes grudging understanding that as stupid and spiteful as these groups often were, they had the absolute right under our constitutional system to the free expression of their ideas.

It was gospel. Our parents and teachers told us that without this freedom, our other freedoms were meaningless. "Freedom of speech is a principal pillar of a free government," wrote Benjamin Franklin. "When this support is taken away, the constitution of a free society is dissolved." Without the ability to say what you like about the political order of the day, your rights to assembly, due process, free worship, and all the rest don't add up to much. Free speech is the linchpin. Free speech is the American religion. "[I]f Men are to be precluded from offering their Sentiments on a matter, which may involve the most serious and alarming consequences," said George Washington in an address to his officers in March 1783, "[then] reason is of no use to us; the freedom of Speech may be taken away, and, dumb and silent we may be led, like sheep, to the slaughter."

Until quite recently, young people were the most reliable champions of unrestricted free speech. Baby boomers launched the modern free speech movement during the 1960s in response to Jim Crow and the U.S. involvement in Vietnam. Gen Xers didn't have anything as dramatic as those causes to raise our voices about, but we did laugh in unison at Tipper Gore's moralistic Parents Music Resource Center, which slapped warning labels on albums to alert parents that their children were listening to civilization-corroding musical compositions such as Prince's "Purple Rain." The PMRC was widely viewed by teenagers in the mid-to-late 1980s as a ham-handed censorship crusade. No one who actually listened to and appreciated popular music took seriously for a second the idea that violent, pornographic, or misogynistic lyrics on a rap album posed a threat to the fabric of society, or that Ozzy Osbourne's latest record contained hidden satanic messages that could drive a borderline personality to suicide. It was all the kind of drummed-up, old-fogey nonsense that had sent censors and scolds after Lenny Bruce in the early 1960s.

The goody-goodies of the PMRC claimed they were only looking to protect children with their tut-tutting and finger wagging, but as Frank Zappa testified before the Senate Commerce, Science, and Transportation Committee in 1985, the PMRC's warning labels wouldn't do much to protect kids while infringing "the civil liberties of people who are not children." The sight of Zappa, folk singer John Denver, and Twisted Sister's Dee Snider giving sworn testimony alongside then-Senator Al Gore was too much to be believed. Or at least so thought everyone I went to high school with. The same was true of the attempts to silence the shock jock Howard Stern. Kids knew he had a right to be as gross and outrageous as he could get away with on the radio, just as we knew that it was our parents' job, not the government's, to police our listening habits. The whole thing was downright stupid and un-American.

These days the young people are positively begging for the authorities to police what people hear and listen to. A 2015 Pew Research Center study found that 40 percent of those between the ages of 18 and 34 felt that the federal government ought to censor potentially offensive statements about minority groups. "Roughly two-thirds of college students say colleges should be allowed to establish policies that restrict slurs and other language that is intentionally offensive to certain groups (69%), as well as the wearing of costumes that stereotype certain racial or ethnic groups (63%)," according to a 2016 Gallup survey. Nearly half of respondents said that they thought that there could be some "legitimate reasons" to prevent the press from covering campus protests.

Rare is the month that goes by without some illiberal mob of college students shouting down a visiting speaker, usually with the active encouragement of their more radical professors. Mostly the targets of these protests are political conservatives, but not always. Student reporters trying to cover 2015 protests regarding the treatment of black students at the University of Missouri were bullied and threatened. That same year, unhinged Yale students surrounded and berated the sociologist and physician Professor Nicholas Christakis after his wife, Erika, herself a teacher at the Ivy League university, had encouraged students to exercise their own judgment regarding the administration's guidelines on potentially offensive Halloween costumes. The Christakises' mistake? Believing that millennials were capable of hearing and understanding an argument that challenged received wisdom about diversity, tolerance, intersectionality, and the culture of offense. Erika Christakis lost her job at Yale for suggesting that students could think and speak for themselves. Needless to say, she and her husband are not right-wingers.

Evergreen State College Professor Bret Weinstein, a self-proclaimed progressive, was hounded out of his job in 2017 for daring to criticize an event that asked white students to absent themselves from the school's Washington State campus for a day. Another self-described progressive, Middlebury College Professor Allison Stanger, was physically attacked after an event she was supposed to moderate with the conservative writer Charles Murray. She had been planning to ask him some "hard questions" about his controversial scholarship on race and social class, but the Middlebury students weren't having it.

"Can you just listen for one minute," Professor Stanger pleaded prior to the attack.

"No!" came the students' thunderous reply.

As she and Murray fled to a waiting car, they were chased and surrounded. Someone in the mob pulled Professor Stanger's hair. She suffered injuries to her neck. Afterward she claimed that she had feared for her life.

All of this happened in the United States of America. In 2017. No student was suspended or expelled for participating in what was essentially a violent Maoist mob.

A 2017 Brookings survey of college students codified with data what the aforementioned episodes had already quite clearly demonstrated: freedom of speech is not a widely supported concept among the tail end of the millennial cohort. "A surprisingly large fraction of students believe it is acceptable to act—including resorting to violence—to shut down expression they consider offensive," wrote the study's author, John Villasenor, who canvassed the opinions of 1,500 college students. Nearly 20 percent of students told Villasenor that shutting down a speaker with violence was a fine thing to do. That means that 1 in 5 college kids think there's nothing wrong with knocking out someone like Erika Christakis, Allison Stanger, Bret Weinstein, Charles Murray, or me, for that matter, in order to keep someone else from having to hear a controversial or contrary viewpoint. Among male students the percentage was higher—30 percent.

Once upon a time, and a very good time it was, the American concept of free speech was celebrated on campus—and among the young, generally—for its unique ability to shame the powerful and challenge orthodoxies. Now tolerance for the expression of a multiplicity of abhorrent, profane, and politically unorthodox views is considered evidence of a bias toward existing unequal systems and institutions. Free speech has become the object of slander, suspicion, scorn, and outright attack.

How did we get here? How is it that the Internet age, which many thought would usher in an unprecedented era of widely proliferating speech and democracy-enriching debate, has in fact descended into a cesspool of politically correct conformity, safe spaces, trigger warnings, speech codes, preferred pronouns, witch hunts, and mob violence? And how is it that it isn't the old fogeys calling for restrictions on speech, but the young, the so-called "digital natives" who are meant to usher us into our glorious online future?

Anyone who doubts that we are headed for a painful generational reckoning on the speech issue ought to consider the frequency with which people lose their jobs after a single misstep on social media. Say the wrong thing on Twitter and some stranger is very likely to contact your employer and demand your head on a platter. Companies no longer have any appetite for defending free speech. Neither do schools, clubs, churches, temples, or government agencies. If the online mob turns its attention your way, you may not even be able to count on the support of your friends and family.

The millennials' love affair with the fuzzy concept of social justice has led many to the warped conclusion that free speech has the power to oppress people rather than liberate them. Witness the saddest development associated with the punitive millennial attitude toward "offensive" speech—the war on humor. As standups from Lenny Bruce to Richard Pryor to Amy Schumer have demonstrated, humor exists on the border between the socially acceptable and the socially abhorrent. Things that we think but aren't allowed to say make us laugh.

Is it wrong to chuckle at our impolitic foibles and private peccadilloes, the little things we know to be true but dare not say? No, it isn't wrong. On the contrary, it keeps us whole. It prevents us from becoming too distant and disconnected from our common humanity. Laughter is the release valve of high-pressure social tension. It gives us an opportunity to pause, look at ourselves, glance over at our neighbors—the otherwise nice guy with the all-wrong politics or the seemingly saintly gal with the irrational prejudices—and bust a healthy gut in mutual recognition of our shortcomings and imperfections.

In the late 1980s the comedian Andrew "Dice" Clay shocked America with his brash, vulgar, and hyper-macho stage act. He specialized in pornographic revisions of children's nursery rhymes, such as Old Mother Hubbard and Hickory Dickory Dock, which he recited in an exaggerated Brooklyn tough-guy accent while puffing ostentatiously on his cigarette. It was clearly an act, but its purpose was oddly hard to discern. Was it satire, social commentary, or simply filth? On the face of it, the Diceman's routine had no redeeming social value, to borrow a phrase much beloved by my father. Some said it was meant as a send-up of the Italianate machismo so often on display in mob movies. Some said that Clay himself wasn't really like that. He was actually kind of a sweet guy. Who knows?

All most people knew was that a lot of the Diceman's jokes were stupid, a few were worth a groan and an eye-roll, and one or two were genuinely funny in a totally out-of-bounds way. If they weren't funny, Clay would never have managed to survive and thrive in the cutthroat stand-up comedy world. This is one of the purest free markets ever to have existed. It has a single price signal—the laugh. The laugh's source is mysterious. It does not derive from supply and demand, as prices in economic markets do. It derives from something impossible to lasso or explain. If something is funny, it makes you laugh. If it isn't, it doesn't. Comedy is a binary thing: yes or no. Up or down. Black or white. Funny or not.

Professional stand-up comics will tell you that figuring out what's funny and what's not is a messy process. No one can say for sure whether a joke will be deemed offensive or hilarious until it's told to an audience. You have to road-test it. Getting it right involves a period of refinement. You need to dance all over the red lines of acceptable public speech in order to find the sweet spot, the laugh. Just like in Silicon Valley, which venerates failure as the necessary precondition for success, comedians can't get better without risking complete humiliation. No risk, no reward.

At least, that's the way it's always been. Things have changed over the past 10 years. A comedian who makes a borderline joke about a protected class of people in 2018 will instantly regret it. Many of the highly regarded stand-ups working today are Gen Xers: Dave Chappelle, Sarah Silverman, Chris Rock, Marc Maron, Jim Gaffigan, and, before his fall from grace, Louis C.K. These comedians, reared during a different time, are the canaries in the free-speech coal mine. In 2015, Rock told *New York* magazine's Frank Rich that he wouldn't play college campuses anymore because the millennial audiences he encountered there were so obsessed with not offending anyone—or being offended—that they couldn't laugh. He went so far as to call them "conservative," which is perhaps the first time a group of 20-year-old college sophomores have been painted with that particular broad brush. Jerry Seinfeld has expressed a similar disinterest in performing on campus, where the disease of political correctness has deprived an entire generation of their collective sense of humor.

Can you imagine Andrew "Dice" Clay reciting one of his nursery rhymes on a college campus today? I doubt you can. In August 2017, websites ranging from Jezebel.com to BET.com ran splashy headlines on stories accusing Dave Chappelle of telling "transphobic jokes." As a Gen Xer I found nothing inherently wrong with that. All I really wanted to know was: were they funny?

Millennials are known far and wide as digital natives. When they are presented that way, it's implied that their facility with Internet-era technology equips them better than any other generation to navigate a future in which constant disruptive innovation is the only certain thing. But is it really such a blessing to be a digital native? I'm not convinced that we should be celebrating it. Given millennials' antipathy toward free speech, it might be more accurate to call them "digital Maoists." Given what we know about the effects of the Internet on the neural pathways of our brains, it might be more accurate to call them "digital junkies."

Strung out and desperate for a fix, millennials can't go long without a deep drink of the mother's milk of the Internet.

I don't mean to suggest that Generation X is disease-free. We have a touch of it, too. We're also losing our appetite for free expression. We have our stupid heads buried in our stupid phones and stupid iPads just like everybody stupid else. We text while we're driving and all that jazz. But, still, we are different, because we remember what it was like before. We're not digital natives, we're digital latecomers. For us, the analog world is still within reach. We remember. In memory there is hope.

SIX

Near Wild Heaven

During the mid-1990s, while Gen Xers were in their twenties, the Internet revolution was just kicking off. A quarter of a century later, that revolution is still in full swing. What it all means remains an open question. The Internet and its associated technologies are changing how we live in ways that no one fully understands (no matter how much they claim to). Everything is metamorphosing. From commerce to communication and from how we drive to how we think, the old ways are disappearing. Some of that change is for the good; some not. The one thing you can say about all of it is that it's happening incredibly fast.

Uber-millennial Mark Zuckerberg dreamed up Facebook in his dorm room at Harvard University in 2004. In 2006, the social-media service began offering accounts to anyone aged 13 or older. In 2016, a mere 12 years after the site was conjured into being, Facebook announced that it had surpassed 1.65 billion monthly active users. In June 2017, they revised upward—2 billion.

As of May 2016, nearly half of Americans were getting their news from Facebook, even as traditional newsgathering organizations were folding up shop and laying off staff. In addition to its mysterious timeline algorithms, the company now employs a cadre of worker bees to "curate" the stories that appear on the site. In November 2016, Facebook announced that it would ban websites that peddle "fake news" from using its advertising platform. Facebook's team of censors trawl the site day and night looking for content they deem hate speech, fake news, slurs, and calls to violence. In September 2017 it emerged that the site had sold hundreds of thousands of dollars' worth of advertising to shady accounts originating in Russia who wallpapered the site with stories intended to influence the outcome of the Trump vs. Clinton contest. That same month Facebook admitted that it was cooperating with congressional investigators and a special counsel looking into potential foreign interference in the 2016 presidential election.

It goes without saying that Facebook has the right to police its property. You and I are under no obligation to use the site. But the fact is that most of us do, and with so many of us getting so much of our news from Facebook, there is another way of looking at its housekeeping efforts: a company that no one had ever heard of a decade and a half ago, and that is still run mostly by millennials—who at least one Silicon Valley entrepreneur describes as "scuzzy"—has granted itself extraordinary and unprecedented censorial power over the news we consume. As if that weren't enough, it now seems as if Zuckerberg, who will be 36 in 2020, is preparing to run for president. He has been touring the country, visiting state fairs and the like, posting photos and stories about his encounters with "regular people."

Facebook is a behemoth corporation, the kind of outfit that people used to worry about having too much influence over individuals and the political economy. "No company better exemplifies the Internet-age dictum that if the product is free, you are the product," wrote John Lanchester in the *London Review of Books*. "Facebook's customers aren't the people who are on the site: its customers are the advertisers who use its network and who relish its ability to direct ads to receptive audiences."

It's not a secret. Fifteen years into the social-media experiment, we can no longer claim ignorance about Facebook's attitude and business model. Still—whether baby boomer, Gen Xer, millennial, or the teenagers that psychologist Jean Twenge calls iGen—we somehow can't resist logging in. We go right on shoveling wheelbarrow after wheelbarrow of our most personal information into Facebook's insatiable maw.

Facebook knows our politics, our tastes in food, our religious affiliations, and our sexual orientations. It knows who our friends and enemies are. It has developed taxonomies of our family relationships and work histories. It can identify us by sight, using digital face-recognition technology to analyze our photos, and tracks us everywhere we go on the Internet. It sells everything it learns about us to its true clients, the advertisers. And yet, somehow, Facebook feels like it isn't getting enough from us. Like a jealous lover, it wants to keep us from talking to its rivals. It wants to stop us from engaging in even the most casual dalliances with Amazon, Apple, Microsoft, and Google. Facebook wants to be our everything.

The rest of the Silicon Valley behemoths have the same attitude. Apple wants us never to leave its beautifully designed closed universe. Its iTunes store and iMusic service are exclusive arrangements. You can't play what you buy there on other devices or other platforms. It's all Apple, only Apple. When Steve Jobs and his engineers invented the iPhone in 2007, we didn't even know we wanted it; now—*a decade later*—we find we can't live without it. By 2014, Apple had sold 590 million of its magical devices worldwide. Just two years later, in August 2016, the company announced that it had sold its billionth iPhone. By contrast, Alexander Graham Bell invented the telephone in 1877. By the time the first transatlantic call was placed 49 years later in 1926, there were just 12 million traditional telephones in service.

The pace of technological change is accelerating at an accelerating rate. If you consider how eager we have demonstrated ourselves to be to adopt any and all time-saving technologies—even when the price is some once-essential life skill or once-valued human interaction—it's hard not to see the danger that Neil Postman, Nicholas Carr, and David McCullough have seen. Drone deliveries, driverless cars, and smart vacuum cleaners are just the beginning. Sex robots are here already. Nonhuman armies are on the horizon. Could self-aware artificial-intelligence systems of the sort dreamed up by James Cameron in 1991's *Terminator 2* be far off?

Don't count on it. Digital winter is coming.

Before arriving at that dead-end future, however, we all will be forced to attend a great many small funerals along the way. With their heads buried in their screens and devices, our kids and grandchildren may never have the experience of going into a store to shop. They may never learn how to read a map, look up a word in a dictionary, cook a meal for themselves, or find a book on a library shelf. They may opt not to mix and mingle in social settings for the purpose of finding a date—a scenario that is already more common than Gen Xers and baby boomers believe or understand. They will certainly never use a wrench and a rag to tinker with the engine of a used car. Those days are already gone; the auto industry went digital a decade ago.

In just a few years' time, many of us may choose not to read anything longer than a tweet. Not that we won't want to, but we won't know how to—our brains won't cooperate. We will forgo the opportunity to see a play live in the theater, hear a band play live music, or visit an art gallery to see a painting in person. All of this will soon be done virtually, in high definition and in the comfort of our own homes, without the bother of getting dressed, getting to a venue, interacting with crowds, and getting home. Just strap a digital scuba mask onto your face and virtual reality will take you there.

People are now using Internet-enabled devices that they never imagined would exist in ways that were never imagined possible just a few short years ago. Some of these improvements are salutary, at least at first glance. Via the so-called Internet of Things, you can preheat your oven or crank the heat in your house while sitting in traffic, miles away from home, so that you can be comfortable after a long trip and get dinner made in a jiff. Fine; on the face of it, this is something to cheer about. You can also check in on your sleeping baby through a wireless video monitor connected to an app on your smartphone. That sounds good, too, until you imagine someone hacking your home network and spying on you or frightening your baby with devilish noises.

Using a digital assistant such as Amazon Echo to order a half-pound bag of Peanut M&M's and some new sneakers while doing sit-ups in your bedroom might seem the epitome of futuristic multitasking, but it's actually a seismic shift in the way we use technology—and the way it uses us. Digital technology is doing more than just changing how we interact with our friends and neighbors; it's changing the way we consume and process news and information, and the way we think. Our minds are literally adapting to the devices we use. It's not at all certain that the long-term effects on our brains will be positive. In fact, I think we can be fairly certain that it is doing us serious harm.

Consider what's happened to romance. The first time I asked a girl to go out with me, I did it by passing her a note in the hallway of

Frelinghuysen Junior High School. I think I was 12, but I may have been 13. The "ask," as they say in business school, was a success. The young lady accepted (also via note), and we immediately became boyfriend and girlfriend—there were no romantic half measures in those days, if I recall—but very little about the transaction had actually been left to chance. The entire exchange had been vetted and approved in advance via eye contact, body language, and the facilitating assistance of friendly intermediaries. Reputation-wise there was a lot to lose from a rejection.

In later years, like young men have done from time immemorial, I summoned the courage to put "the ask" into spoken words. Sometimes this took the form of a well-rehearsed and nerve-crushing phone call, numbers punched by fingers attached to hands with sweaty palms. "Hi, can Jenny come to the phone?" Occasionally it was accomplished via face-to-face conversation in the hallway of Morristown High School or near the visitor-side bleachers of the football field. Almost always the outcome was foreordained, though that never seemed to make the act of stepping up to the plate any less terrifying.

The demands of this particular social ritual were well understood by me, as they were by every young man of Generation X. You had to ask. You had to put it into words. You had to "grow a pair"—do they say that in business school?—and conquer your fears. Without facing down your terror of being rejected, you would be consigned to a lifetime of loneliness, bitter explanations, and blustery excuses. You would stay home while everyone else went to the dance. The equation was simple: no guts, no glory. No ask, no date.

It felt good. The accomplishment of facing my social fears and coming away with a victory was edifying. Standing up and confronting the world, eyeball-to-eyeball, is a big part of life, and getting some wins under your belt at a young age, while the stakes are still relatively low, is character-building. On the female side of the equation, the ritual was just as well understood. A guy who couldn't summon the courage to ask you to the dance was probably not worth your time. Some nervous fumbling can be endearing, but experience has taught me that few women, young or old, find paralyzing social anxiety attractive. I've heard from some women that the fear of being asked out by a boy who had somehow mistaken a polite hallway smile for a great big green light could occasionally be stressful. Yet for the most part, as the old saying goes, "It's nice to be asked." Even when forced to scramble for a plausible excuse as to why they just can't accept an invitation to the movies—not tonight, tomorrow, or anytime, really, before graduation—most young women would rather be invited out than ignored.

I know young adults whose pulses race uncontrollably at the thought of placing a phone call to a landlord, lawyer, plumber, or doctor. The idea of a job interview reduces their insides to a pile of quivering jelly. Maybe they are by nature anxious about interacting with the world. Mostly I think their problems stem from how they were nurtured. No one ever encouraged them to grapple with their fears. Maybe they were purposely insulated from difficult social exchanges. Maybe they never felt confident enough in their swing to step up to the plate and take a live pitch. It's not only a pity; it's counterproductive. Embarrassment has its social purpose. Crashing and burning once in a while (if you're a guy) or fielding the occasional unsolicited, unwanted offer (if you're a gal) can help you develop a healthy sense of who's who and what's what on the uneven terrain of interpersonal relations. When it comes to delivering and interpreting social cues, young women and young men need practice. Experience is the best teacher.

Who knew that "asking someone out" would so quickly become as quaint and old-fashioned as a chaperoned stroll along a pleasant country lane? According to Pew, between 2014 and 2016, the use of online dating services and mobile apps tripled among 18–24-year-olds. The biggest of these services have become household names: eHarmony, Tinder, Match, OkCupid. But savvy millennials know that there are plenty of others to choose from—Bumble, Hinge, the unusually named Coffee Meets Bagel. About 1 in 5 young people have a dating app on their phones; 1 in 6 say they are "addicted" to hunting for love by swiping right and swiping left.

I see no reason to declare that the phenomenon of online dating is a disaster for humanity. Quite a few long-lasting couples of my acquaintance have met that way. But the popularity of these services has undoubtedly altered the landscape of romantic interactions. A guy no longer needs to grow a pair and step up to the plate. A gal no longer needs to look a guy in the eye when she rejects his proposal. They both can simply swipe right if they like what they see in a profile photo and swipe left if they don't—no different than choosing a new sweater.

Associated dating phenomena and behaviors have grown up around the left-right-swipe culture. "Benching" and "breadcrumbing" involve stringing along a romantic prospect for an inconsiderate amount of time while you nose around online for someone better. "Cushioning" refers to keeping one eye on what's happening on the apps while you are involved in an active relationship in real life. It's a hedge in case things don't quite take off with your current paramour.

If you haven't heard these terms, it's a good bet you're not a millennial. I'm personally in a happy marriage, and have been for 16 years, so I'm not in the best position to evaluate the social value of these trends. I've never used an online dating site or app. I hope I never will. However, if you've made it this far into the book, it won't surprise you to learn that I'm somewhat bearish on the whole damn thing. As metaphors for what the Internet has done to us, "swipe right" and "swipe left" are about as distressingly useful as they come. Shallow, transactional, selfish, and anonymous, the online dating culture seems a pure reflection of the damage the Internet is capable of doing—and is doing. As a recent article in the *Wall Street Journal* pointed out, online dating has scrambled even the most basic elements of a first date. No one even knows who is supposed to pay anymore, the man or the woman.

Can you imagine being a teenager today? You'd never be able to fool your parents about where you'd been or whom you'd been with. You'd never be able to watch a program on TV that you maybe weren't supposed to watch—digital detectives can find out, even post hoc, what's been going on in your Netflix queue. Every party you go to gets documented on social media. Breaking up with a boyfriend or a girlfriend is no longer a private pain, a rite of personal passage, or an opportunity for necessary emotional growth and introspection. No, it's a public drama. Your entire school community gets instantly notified. So does your soccer team and so do your friends from summer camp who live in another state. Worse, there's no longer any wondering whether your ex-paramour has moved on. Unless you unfriend or block them on social media, you'll be treated to updates on all of their latest romantic exploits. Whether those exploits are real or staged just for the purpose of torturing you, well, you'll never know that, so I suppose I was partly wrong; even in the digital age, being a teenager retains at least some of its mysterious danger.

Like I said in Chapter Four, Neil Postman wouldn't have been surprised by any of it. His books *Amusing Ourselves to Death* (1985) and *Technopoly* (1993) updated and extended Marshall McLuhan's influential theories on media. Where McLuhan declared that "the medium is the message," Postman added a twist. The medium, he wrote, is a metaphor: "The form in which ideas are expressed affects what those ideas will be." It doesn't matter if the available medium is the Internet, the printing press, the television, the telegraph, the alphabet, or merely verbal speech. Each medium has a "bias," in Postman's words, that "sits heavily, felt but unseen, over a culture." A purely oral culture will develop—legally, culturally, social, economically, *romantically*—in a particular and unique way due, in part, to the organizing logic of the spoken word. Proverbs and custom will hold sway, whereas in a culture whose dominant technology is the printing press, legal texts such as Magna Carta or the American Constitution naturally hold sway.

In a culture dominated by pocket-sized telephones with more individual computing power than NASA used in the 1960s to send the Apollo astronauts to the moon, we might expect to see exactly what we are seeing—people falling into potholes on the street because they can't take their eyes off their glowing screens; glassy-eyed teenagers choosing to spend the bulk of their time in online cocoons playing virtual-reality games against opponents they've never met; marriageable young men and women opting for the convenient disposability of pornography rather than a meaningful (and perhaps messy) emotional entanglement with a mate; and a broad and rapid decline in general knowledge because you can "just look it up."

Technology surrounds our ideas, infiltrates and distorts them, and ultimately shapes our ability to express them. "[I]n every tool we create," Postman observes, "an idea is embedded that goes beyond the function of the thing itself." An online dating app that encourages us to approach the selection of our romantic partners in the same way we approach the selection of our wardrobes is eventually going to have some undesirable effects on our ability to sustain healthy relationships. Tell me you don't see it happening everywhere you turn.

In the Internet world, the bias that sits heavy but unseen over the culture is relativity. Everything is temporary, so nothing is important. Everything is sort of casual, so everything is sort of meaningless. Every dopey thing a celebrity does is a front-page story, so nothing is news. Everything is OMG The Biggest Crisis Ever, so nothing really matters. I'll be the first one to admit that the election of a president who shuns the traditional methods of communicating with the American people has been a disaster very much in line with what Postman would have predicted. And I'm as sure as I've ever been of anything that Trump's tendency to tweet his thoughts and policy decisions has added gallons and gallons of fuel to what was already an uncontainable cultural wildfire. His view of the truth as an obstacle to his self-fulfillment hasn't helped matters. But I'm equally convinced that Donald Trump is a symptom of our disease, not its cause.

The Trump presidency and all its violent ructions are in some sense the natural byproducts of the society we have all been building these past 10 or 15 years—aggressive, inconsiderate, disconnected, selfish, distracted, profane. I suppose we should be surprised that the rot reached the highest office in the land as quickly as it did, but as I have been pointing out, the pace of change is accelerating at an accelerating rate. Perhaps it takes a political disruption on the scale of the Trump presidency for the tech industry's uncritical cheerleaders to throw their hands up and say, "Whoa, wait a minute. Maybe we should slow this runaway train down."

In 2012, long before his excommunication from polite society, Louis C.K. did a bit on *Conan* that achieved rare notoriety in an age when late-night TV viewership was at a nadir. It's become known as "Everything's Amazing, and Nobody's Happy." The comedian satirizes an airline passenger enraged that he can't get a signal on his cell phone as the plane hurtles through the skies above the earth at 30,000 feet. The flier has access to more and better technology than almost every human being who has ever walked the face of the earth, and still he's deeply offended to the point of cursing and stomping his feet when the inflight WiFi cuts out on him. "We live in an amazing world, and it's wasted on the crappiest generation of spoiled idiots," Louis C.K. joked.

In 2012 it was a new and amusing observation on the emerging state of things. Now it seems sadly prophetic.

SEVEN

(I Always Feel Like) Somebody's Watching Me

Lloyd Dobler is a hero. The 18-year-old high school graduate played by John Cusack in the 1989 romantic comedy *Say Anything* has an awkward charm about him that many Gen Xers admire. During his teen-comedy heyday, Cusack excelled at this particular type. Lloyd is a wiseacre with a soft heart. He is effortlessly cool. He can handle himself verbally. He has a sense of humor and an inherent goodness. Most important, he clearly wants to move from being a teenager to being an adult without compromising his idealism or integrity. This is something to which most young people can relate. In this, millennials are no different from any generation that came before.

A kickboxing fanatic, Lloyd loves Diane Court, an academic super-star played by the willowy actress Ione Skye. At a somewhat formal dinner party at Diane's home, her deeply skeptical father puts the nervous Lloyd on the spot. What are his plans now that high school is over? Diane is headed off to college—Oxford, no less. What is Lloyd planning to do with his life? The answer doesn't seem to impress the unyielding, gravel-voiced Mr. Court, played with rare pathos by the late John Mahoney, but Lloyd's commitment to living an authentic and uncorrupted life does impress the viewer, even 30 years later. "I don't want to sell anything, buy anything, or process anything as a career," says Lloyd. "I don't want to sell anything bought or processed, or buy anything sold or processed, or process anything bought, sold, or processed, or repair anything bought, sold, or processed. You know, as a career. I just don't want to do that." It's a comprehensive portfolio of things Lloyd *doesn't want to do.* He concludes by saying he hasn't got it all figured out just yet, so he's just going to "hang" with Diane.

Who doesn't wish they had been that cool at 18?

Lloyd looks and sounds like a teenager, but he is wise beyond his years, a lot like *Say Anything's* wunderkind director, Cameron Crowe, who eventually turned his teenage adventures as a precocious rock journalist into the film *Almost Famous.* In a changing world, the act of drawing lines in the sand can be a matter of survival. Being 18 years old is to live in a changing world. You can lose precious parts of yourself in the chaos of the transition from adolescence to adulthood. Sometimes the best thing a person can know about himself is what he doesn't want to be or become. The places you won't go say as much about you as the places you will.

When it comes to the digital world, Generation X needs to know where it will and won't go. The last analog generation needs to draw a line in the sand, saying clearly, "Here, and no further." The technological hill we should be willing to die on is called the Internet of Things.

It's a big term, encompassing any device that once had a purely analog function but can now be connected to the web. Home appliances are the natural frontier. Ovens, fridges, washing machines, dryers, vacuums, thermostats, and other key tools of modern living have already been wired up. But the existence of the Internet of Things has provided a rationale for the development of new products—the kinds of things that were previously the stuff of dreams.

The hugely popular Amazon Echo, aka Alexa, is a wireless voice-recognition tool that sits in your house and waits patiently for you to give it an order. Tell it to grab you a few rolls of paper towels, and the Echo will do so on the hop, dinging the credit card you have on file with Amazon Prime, the Seattle-based online retailer's paid subscription service. The paper towels will arrive on your front steps in a day or two. Tell the Echo to hunt down a long-forgotten love song that you used to blast from the stereo of your parents' car when you were 17 and tooling around town with the windows down, and it will cue up the track from

Amazon's Music Unlimited streaming service, which is headquartered in the undefinable digital vapor known as the "cloud." Access to this virtual library containing "tens of millions of songs" is offered ad-free and at a discount to Prime members, who, in exchange for this on-demand cornucopia, pay a modest annual fee entitling them to free home shipping of books and such—if, in fact, you happen to be the kind of Gen X square who still prefers to read books printed on paper. Ask the Echo to answer a trivia question, and it will happily do so free of charge.

The device works by listening for a "wake word" that you, the willing user, have programmed it to recognize. When you say the word—often it is, simply, "Alexa"—the Echo begins recording your voice. It then transmits the recording to a server-processor somewhere out in the cloud. Once your command is safely arrived in the Amazonian cumulonimbus, the algorithms cooked up by the (you hope) benevolent social engineers in Silicon Valley translate it from a voice recording to a string of digital blips and bleeps. This, somehow, helps the billowing data-brain they've constructed determine what it is you actually want to know or buy. Then Amazon acts on that information—the digital DJ spins your best high school jam or a box of paper towels takes the first step on its long journey to your front steps.

If you have an Echo, it means you have already provided Amazon with your credit card number, address, birthday, Christmas list, and, presumably, your deodorant preferences, your spouse's taste in movies, and your baby's diaper size. Funnily enough, market research shows that people don't mind handing over such highly personal information . . . to the right company. According to *Fortune* magazine, Amazon is one of the three most admired companies in the world, along with Apple and Google. What sets these behemoth corporations apart from other tech titans like Facebook, Uber, Tinder, Match, Twitter—or even Visa and Mastercard? All collect, store, and sell your personal information to advertisers, but Amazon, Apple, and Google are perceived as providing a valuable—even essential—service in exchange for the right to monetize your privacy.

I'll pause here to state what I hope is obvious: only the most naïve would assume that Amazon—which has built a billion-dollar global company by anticipating your needs and then delivering on them—will only have your privacy in mind when making business decisions in the future. In 2012, the company filed for and was granted a patent for an "anticipatory package shipping" system that uses an algorithm to predict what you will buy before you actually close the deal. Past shopping history, items stored in your cart on your wish list, stuff that you might have hovered over while browsing the site, and other information the company has learned about you from its marketing and research efforts are all brought together to "predict" what you want to buy when you log on to their site. The purpose is to help Amazon eliminate the one natural advantage that brick-and-mortar stores still have on it—time. It takes a day or two to get those paper towels delivered to your front steps. Yes, Amazon has warehouses and fulfillment centers all around the country. Yes, they recently snapped up Whole Foods and its 400 physical stores. They can get stuff to you pretty darn quickly. But deodorant or baby diapers won't do you very much good tomorrow morning if you really need them tonight.

Do you see now how valuable it might be to Amazon to have some "ears on the ground" providing it with real-time information about your Christmas shopping or exercise habits? Once companies like Amazon have spies in your living room, it will be far easier for them to get a jump on the annual holiday shipping crunch. Amazon has been tight-lipped about the exact number of Echoes it has sold since the device was introduced in 2014, but at Christmas 2016 the Jeff Bezos–owned company boasted that sales of the device had increased a walloping nine times over the previous year's tally. Alexa is a hot commodity. Google and Apple quickly brought their own versions of the digital butler to market. Google calls its smart speaker Home, while Apple calls its version HomePod.

From the point of view of the average modern electronics consumer, who somewhere in his house has turned a box, closet, or entire room into a graveyard of discarded devices, the Amazon Echo has potential as a technological unifier, combining the functions of several other gadgets and eliminating some of the time, trouble, and friction involved in shopping for stuff. For some it may even be the fulfillment of a fantasy. It's like something out of science fiction. *Star Trek* fans have noted its similarity to the *USS Enterprise*'s computer system, which seemed to be as omniscient as it was benign. But the prospects for Alexa abuse—even if only at the hands of the neighbors' prank-happy children—should be obvious to anyone with a grasp of how the nonfiction world works.

"Because Alexa responds to verbal commands, the Echo is incredibly child-friendly," wrote Alice Truong in June 2016 at QZ.com, a business-focused digital news site. "Unlike the iPad, which children have taken to with ease (ever see a toddler try to swipe a book or TV?), the Amazon Echo doesn't require them to learn new gestures or even know how to read." All they have to know how to do is boss people around—or boss things around, as the case may be. Children are naturally pretty good at making unreasonable demands, but it's a trait that parents used to work hard at undoing.

Not long ago my wife and kids went to a party at the home of some friends who owned an Amazon Echo (and, it should be said, are quite happy with the service it provides). Once my toddler figured out how the device worked, she delighted her hosts by calling for a few tunes to dance and sing along with. Alexa undoubtedly spiced up the party. My daughter's rendition of Eddy Grant's early '80s classic "Electric Avenue" was a hit, but the laughs wore thin when she insisted on repeat plays of José Feliciano's "Feliz Navidad." It was the early spring, many long, grey weeks since the sun had set on the twelfth day of Christmas. She just loves that song. Woe to those who don't when there's an Echo around.

In Dallas, Texas, parents Megan and Michael Neitzel scratched their heads in confusion when a giant box containing a dollhouse and 4 pounds of sugar cookies was delivered to their house. The day before the package arrived their 6-year-old daughter, Brooke, had had what she considered an innocent chat with the family's new Echo Dot, a smaller second-generation version of Alexa. The little girl at first denied placing the $162 order, but eventually fessed up. The Neitzels took it in stride, with Megan telling a local news station, "Technology is moving so fast, and that's a good thing, but we need to stay one step ahead of it as parents." Good advice, but everybody knows how parental attempts to outfox children on the subject of technology usually end. Kids always figure out a way around their parents' defenses. It's one of the immutable laws of the universe.

For its part, Amazon suggested that parents like the Neitzels should add a few layers of protection to their Echo service—like insisting upon a confirmation code for every order or, incredibly, turning off the device's voice-purchasing function. These strategies would seem to undermine the value of having the Echo in your home. That is, if you look at it from the consumer's point of view. From Amazon's point of view, perhaps, getting the Echo Dot through the front door is good enough for now.

According to the ad campaign promoting this household wonder, Amazon encourages you to speak to its machine the way you would speak to a slave:

"Alexa, find me the best deal on a hotel in Amsterdam this summer."

"Alexa, we need a case of seltzer water and an oversize bag of tortilla chips delivered in time for the party on Saturday."

"Alexa, who directed *The Conversation*?"

Parents have already begun to notice that their children don't speak to the device in the politest of tones. Just like royal brats in the nursery at Buckingham Palace, tech-savvy American kids—not big on "please" and "thank you" under ordinary circumstances—have cottoned on to the idea that the device in the corner of the room neither judges your choices nor chides you for insolence. What kid could resist bossing Alexa around? It's not just the children, though. "People do not talk to their dog the way they speak to Alexa," noted one *New York Times* journalist.

Put simply, Alexa is a nightmare for Gen X parents. Already over-stressed by the online revolution and its ever-expanding universe of technologies, networks, apps, and lingo, we now have to worry about a virtual big brother in the house, listening to our every thoughtless utterance and storing it somewhere in the cloud for future use, either for or against us. Worse, everyone from Alec Baldwin, who starred in Super Bowl ads to promote the Echo, to the millennials who work alongside us and who never met a gizmo they didn't like, seems to think the whole idea is just grand.

Alexa's cheerleaders are missing something, or, more probably, are choosing to ignore it. We know how Internet-based companies like Amazon, Facebook, Google, Twitter, and the rest build up dossiers on their users and sell them to advertisers. We know how infrequently these Silicon Valley tech behemoths actually take the initiative to protect our privacy. They do it, but often only when the chorus of voices demanding action grows too loud to ignore. We also know how eager bad guys in Russia, Romania, and Rapid City are to hack into such databases and sweep up our passwords and payment information, and maybe even learn our secret desires for the purposes of blackmail—or worse.

They call voice-recognition technologies like Alexa and Apple's Siri "artificial intelligence," but in truth they aren't that sharp. The Echo—first released in 2014—is actually quite a blunt instrument. A gadget reviewer for the *New York Times* called the Echo "mind-numbingly literal" and quipped that if Alexa were your personal assistant, you'd fire her. And, not to be a buzzkill, but what about the possible legal ramifications of having a "mind-numbingly literal" digital narc in your kitchen? In 2016, a murder suspect in Bentonville, Arkansas, acquiesced to prosecutors' demands to hand over recordings from the Amazon Echo device in his home. Amazon fought the request, citing its desire to protect users' privacy rights. Only when the suspect's lawyer (who, in a twist, starred in *Making a Murderer*, a documentary television series produced by Amazon's streaming rival Netflix) apparently decided that there could be nothing on the tapes that would get his client locked up did the Echo's makers hand over the files. A judge dismissed the case in December 2017.

It was nice of Amazon to cooperate with the authorities, but keep in mind that by initially refusing to play ball, Amazon was essentially running cover for a murder suspect—and in a relatively out-of-the-way place. Would they have shown such a firm commitment to their customer's privacy rights if the murder being investigated had happened in Boston, New York, or Los Angeles, and the attack-dog tabloids in those towns got after Amazon to hand over what it knew to the authorities? Apple found itself in a similar situation in early 2016 when the FBI demanded that the company tell the government how to unencrypt information on the iPhone used by domestic terrorist Syed Farook before his December 2015 attack on the Inland Regional Center in San Bernardino, California. Apple refused the order. Public reaction was split—polls showed that roughly half of Americans supported the government, which ultimately managed to get into the phone without Apple's help by paying hackers to exploit a previously unknown software flaw.[7]

Mass murder and terrorism are big deals, so these cases may not be the best example of the types of sticky wickets that always-listening

---

7 The feds squared off with Apple again after the November 2017 church shooting in Sutherland Springs, Texas, with the FBI alleging that encryption had prevented agents from accessing suspect Devin Kelley's device during the crucial early hours of the investigation. The company quickly issued a statement saying they had offered to "expedite our response" to the FBI's requests for information. Apple and other technology companies must hand over customer

technologies could plant in your backyard. Suppose it isn't a murder that's at issue. How many times have you blown your stack over some petty family foul like the ice tray being left empty, or said something to a friend in the heat of the moment that might not play so well if it were recorded and splashed out of context on the front page of a tabloid newspaper? I'm guessing you can think of more than a few times that you've directed indiscrete or vaguely threatening words at a slowpoke in the lane in front of you or a driver who recklessly cut you off. Your car will be spying on you soon, too, if it isn't already.

Millennials are famous for their unconcern about digital privacy, but one of the great benefits of maintaining a distinction between the public and private spheres is that individuals retain the right to engage in a host of behaviors when they're behind closed doors that they would never dream of engaging in on their front porches or in the town square. You could make a compelling case that without this distinction, society as we know it would pretty rapidly come unglued. Paranoia, fear, predatory opportunism, depression—these are the hallmarks of life in a surveillance state, and that is precisely where we are headed by inviting these corporations to set up listening posts in our living rooms.

Maybe you think I'm being a little dramatic and overstating the dangers that the Amazon Echo potentially poses? It's only a handsome little cylinder, after all, connected to the Internet that we all love and use all day, every day to complete an endless string of harmless and necessary tasks. Like the iPhone, the Echo's elegant simplicity belies what it's capable of, and what it stands for. Until recently, we used the Internet as a tool—a sophisticated one, yes, but *we* used *it*. When we needed it to help us accomplish a real-world goal, like shopping or looking for directions, we switched it on and put it to work. Now, it's the one using us, eternally listening, patiently waiting for a command but all the while—potentially—recording our conversations and tracking our digital footsteps. The truly scary thing about the Internet, and the Internet of Things in particular, is that it's a two-way street: traffic in, traffic out. That's what makes us so vulnerable.

information—including files that have been backed up on cloud servers—in response to warrants, but they have vowed never to help law enforcement unlock a cell phone by bypassing a user's access code or biometric data. Silicon Valley and federal law enforcement authorities seem likely to keep butting heads until one party bends.

In Dallas, Texas, on April 7, 2017, at a few minutes before midnight on a Friday, all 156 of the city's emergency sirens began wailing at once, blaring tones intended to signal an impending civic disaster. More than 4,000 panicky residents called 9-1-1 asking what was going on. Was it a tornado? The skies were clear. Did they need to evacuate? Was it an attack? A fire? A flash flood? Nope, it was just a hacker who had managed to gain control of Big D's Internet-connected emergency-alert system and thought he'd have a little fun. The city's Office of Emergency Management didn't know what to do. They couldn't get into their computers to turn off the sirens, which kept blasting their ear-splitting tones for more than 90 minutes. The hacker had locked them out. Many residents took to Twitter looking for answers. The FBI tweeted: "Emergency sirens in #Dallas are malfunctioning. There is no severe weather in #DFW and no active emergency." In the end, all flustered Dallas officials could do was pull the plug on the whole system.

The Dallas hack bore resemblance to an attack the previous year in San Francisco. Hackers in that city managed to install a malicious virus known as "ransomware" on computers at the city's Municipal Transportation Agency. When the ne'er-do-wells pushed play on their scheme, they managed to seize control of San Francisco's centrally controlled light-rail system, shutting down its fare-gate system and letting riders in for free. The hackers demanded a $70,000 payment to release control of the railway back to the city, but the ransom was never paid. Officials managed to liberate the infected computers in short order and get the trolleys moving again. It was a 24-hour nuisance for San Francisco, but was the attack a harbinger of worse—and creepier—mischief to come?

A Washington State couple named Jay and Sarah (news reports withheld their last names for obvious reasons) grew concerned when their 3-year-old son developed anxiety about going to bed. They didn't know whether to believe the boy when he told them that someone was talking to him at night. "Wake up, little boy," he claimed he'd heard a voice say in the darkness. "Daddy's looking for you." Jay and Sarah thought maybe their son was simply having nightmares, until they went to check on him one night and heard the voice, too. "Look, someone's coming," Jay heard the voice say as he entered his son's room. Someone—somewhere—had hacked their Internet-enabled baby monitor, the kind you can check through an app on your smartphone.

The popularity of Internet-connected security cameras and home alarms has skyrocketed despite regular reports that the systems are easily hijacked. A family in Houston, Texas, was horrified to learn that a live feed from the webcam in their 8-year-old daughter's room had been streaming on the Internet. The girl's mother only found out when a woman in Oregon happened across the livestream while surfing the web. Horrified, that woman decided to try to contact the family. A security company determined that hackers were able to gain access to the webcam because the young victim had innocently entered the name of the household's WiFi server in order to play the online video game Minecraft. What do the bighearted social engineers in Silicon Valley advise you to do in such circumstances? Regularly change your password.

Government spying is a further privacy concern raised by the Internet of Things. In early 2017, the whistleblower website WikiLeaks released a trove of documents purportedly revealing the Central Intelligence Agency's ability to hack your Internet-enabled television set and turn it into a listening device. The same WikiLeaks document dump indicated that the CIA has targeted Apple, designing malware that can infect "factory fresh" iPhones and snoop on users' texts, phone and FaceTime calls, and Siri queries.

"Siri, why do I feel like I'm being watched?"

Not that any of us have mischief on our minds, or are planning on doing something that would make us the target of a CIA spying campaign, but I'm personally mystified by the eagerness with which people of my generation are outfitting their homes with recording devices on a direct two-way line to a behemoth corporation with snooping on its mind. We're already walking around with Global Positioning System devices in our pockets that can be used to verify our whereabouts at any given time. Even as we moan about the helicopter parenting trend that has put so much distance between our own unsupervised, semi-dangerous childhoods and the current overscheduled, surveillance-state version of being a kid, we stick cell phones in our young ones' backpacks so that we'll never not know where they are. Television commercials sell us on the virtues of a car that can be programmed to send you an alert if your teenager tops the speed limit or wanders outside a prescribed range of miles from home.

Tech boosters claim that we are still in the earliest days of the artificial-intelligence era and we shouldn't be too surprised when these gizmos fail to live up to their potential. "The machines will learn as they go" seems to be the argument emanating out of Silicon Valley. "Give them a chance." They may learn as they go, but I'm not convinced that's a good thing. I saw *Blade Runner*. I know what happens when the technology becomes self-aware. I've read *Frankenstein*. I know what happens when the inventor loses control of his invention. Facebook recently got spooked when a pair of experimental robots began inventing their own language in order to carry out a simple task that some engineers had assigned them. The company canceled the trial, which is encouraging. Somebody at the social-media supercollider evidently sees the peril in giving these computers too much freedom and independence. How long will they continue to see it? Am I allowed to ask that question?

The home isn't the only digital frontier within which Silicon Valley seeks to establish an outpost. Your car is a ripe target, too. The risks are similar, if a little more physically dangerous. For at least the last decade, any car you buy has come equipped with a pretty sophisticated computer system on board for diagnostic and repair purposes. Beyond the basics, the average person has no idea how a car works. It's too complicated. There are too many parts, too many systems, too many displays, too many monitors, too many fluids, too many toggles, struts, cams, and pistons for you or me to wrap our basic little minds around. We bring our cars to experts to fix. Because we have no idea what they do—and the experts know it—we are often at their mercy. They can charge essentially whatever they want. Who hasn't taken a car in for routine maintenance and left with the feeling that a crime had occurred?

For years, your auto mechanic was a super-smart guy who was great with his hands but probably wasn't on the college track in high school. As his customer, you hoped he was at heart an honest fellow, padding his bill with no more than what he chiseled out of everybody else. He may have been a teensy bit of a grafter, but he had a human face. You could tell when he was lying to you, or you thought you could. If his charm wore thin, you could try your luck with a different mechanic whose personality and rates better suited your tastes.

Who will be your auto mechanic in the era of the self-driving, Internet-connected car? It won't be Randy "Big Dandy" Robertson from high school. It will be a lovely sounding fellow in a call center in Bangalore who talks you gently and respectfully through the rebooting of your car's digital systems. Car maintenance will resemble computer maintenance—that is, you will now be entirely at the mercy of remote, monotonal, and maddeningly un-ruff-able customer-service agents. Before long, they, too, will be replaced by artificial intelligence.

"Siri, why is there smoke coming out of the dashboard?"

The wiring up of automobiles to the Internet is a trend that should be of special concern to those watching out for the erosion of privacy rights, not to mention safety. Turning cars into computers on wheels has exposed them to previously unheard-of vulnerabilities. It used to be you could only get carjacked late at night in a bad neighborhood. Now you can have your high-powered luxury car turned instantly into a junkyard jalopy by a MacBook mastermind in Siberia, or even closer to home.

In 2015, a *WIRED* journalist volunteered to test the ability of a pair of hackers to carjack a Jeep Cherokee while it cruised on the Interstate at 70 miles per hour. With the digital desperadoes ensconced in a safe house 10 miles away, writer Andy Greenberg navigated onto a highway on the edge of St. Louis, Missouri. Without warning, his volunteer attackers began remotely controlling the car's functions. They cranked the air-conditioning and ran the windshield wipers. They tuned the radio to a hip-hop station and blasted the volume—laughing all the way. His eardrums thrumming, Greenberg bashed at the knobs to no avail.

Then the coup de grace: they cut the transmission. "As I frantically pressed the pedal and watched the RPMs climb, the Jeep lost half its speed, then slowed to a crawl," recalled Greenberg. "This occurred just as I reached a long overpass, with no shoulder to offer an escape. The experiment had ceased to be fun." The machines may, indeed, learn as they go, but who can say for sure what the body count will be before HAL graduates into competence?

Maybe I was wrong when I said the Internet is a two-way street. It's actually a 66-lane highway going in both directions, with on-ramps and off-ramps on each lane—a blur of speeding traffic, dangerous drivers, and confusing street signs.

Here's what it comes down to: you don't need the Internet of Things. You think you do because everyone else is slowly getting on board with the idea of a coffee pot that orders its own filters or a fridge that tells you when you're running low on butter. In fact, you don't require Internet-connected devices in your home; none of us do. We have had lovely lives, for the most part, without the "help" of these digital butlers. We had good relationship with our cars without ever having to ask them to drive themselves for a few miles while we answered a phone call or fed a bottle to a baby. You wouldn't offer a spare bedroom in your house to a friend you knew was reporting your movements and habits to a big corporation, would you? Why would you let your minivan and your coffee pot do essentially the same thing?

Cars have worked just fine for the past 100 years without being connected to the Internet. So have thermostats, baby monitors, stoves, boilers, lawn sprinklers, and picture frames. What more is necessary? The promised luxury of self-driving, self-navigating, self-confident cars is no more necessary than a toothbrush that tells you when you need to see the dentist. You can count 6 months. You know what your responsibilities are. Stop off-loading them onto inanimate objects and allegedly smart devices.

You don't need an Alexa, Google Home, Apple HomePod, or any smart device that sits in your house and listens to your conversations all day trying to suss out your secret desires and act on them before you can. How long before "Alexa, I think we need more toilet paper" becomes "Matthew, I think you're using too much toilet paper." The foolishness knows no bounds, yet these contraptions are flying off the shelves. It's worth a reminder that the Internet is not a safe space—or even a private one. It's a public space, where the person (or, rather, the big corporation) supplying you with the right of entry and exit is also snooping on you constantly, tracking your every move, storing information about you in a gigantic database, and selling it to other behemoth corporations. It's like East Germany with kick-ass customer service.

The grand bargain between Silicon Valley and the average person has been—and will continue to be—this: you give up your privacy and we'll give you cool stuff. It's not stuff that anyone needs, really. It's stuff that wows; stuff that makes you gasp at the creativity, the ingenuity, and the sheer gall of the people who dreamt it up. Is it nice to have a GPS-enabled phone in your pocket that takes photos, calls cabs, texts, e-mails, orders food, makes reservations, and helps you find a home? Yes. But it's not anything that you can't live without. In some cases it's making you crazy, and, as we've seen in earlier chapters, it's making you dumb.

Privacy, they say, is something that future generations won't care about. In an earlier technological age, people worried about airing their family's "dirty laundry" in public. Reasonable people understood that the injunction to "mind their own business" was always underpinned by a shared belief that anyone had the absolute right to tell you to butt out of their private affairs at any time. Few people under the age of 30 think anyone has their own business to mind anymore. But this is mere glib reflection. The real problem is much more serious.

Millennials have already made peace with the idea that they won't have any privacy. In fact, they've learned to love the idea that nothing is off-limits, everything is for public consumption, and everyone is always on display. For a millennial, we are told, life is a kind of online competition to see who can post the most glamorous photos or the most savagely clever political retort. I've had millennials tell me they don't care what Google or Amazon or Facebook knows about them, because they've got nothing to hide and these companies are only keeping such close tabs on their customers so they can refine and expedite the products and services on offer. A 2015 survey by the American Press Institute found just 20 percent of millennials worried "a good deal" or "most of the time" about online privacy. The vast majority said they never worried or only worried a little about how much searchable personal information about them was available on the Internet. Why such nonchalance among the digital natives about their privacy? "They believe that everyone is going to know everything eventually anyway," said one high school teacher.

In his 2016 book *The Inevitable: Understanding the 12 Technological Forces That Will Shape Our Future*, the noted technology guru and *WIRED* magazine founder Kevin Kelly had this to say:

> If today's social media has taught us anything about ourselves as a species, it is that the human impulse to share overwhelms the human impulse for privacy. This has surprised the experts. So far, at every juncture that offers a choice, we've tilted, on average, toward more sharing, more disclosure, more transparency. I would sum it up like this: Vanity trumps privacy.

Don't buy it—don't buy any of it. Fight for your privacy. Fight to be left alone. Like Lloyd Dobler, fight for your right to be uncorrupted by commercial intrusions on your life's plan. Fight to get the old way of living back, the one in which no one was reading your mail or spying on your coffee consumption. Resist the Internet of Things. It's a violent reversal of the long-standing distinction between the public sphere and the private sphere. Take the threat seriously.

EIGHT

Great Big No

By this point it should come as no surprise that I view the entire Silicon Valley–directed artificial-intelligence program to be something of a conspiracy. It's a soft conspiracy, true, with no single puppet master pulling all the strings all the time, but it's a conspiracy nonetheless in that it hopes to achieve a specific outcome through the use of objectively surreptitious means. The goal is to break our connection with—and affinity for—the rapidly receding world of books, letters, patience, and character, of which Generation X will soon be the last Americans with any memory.

The conspirators are the big tech companies that we all know (and some we don't), the global manufacturing sector, the auto industry, the government (to a greater or lesser degree, depending on who's in charge), and—let's face it—us. That would be you, me, and just about everyone we know. We've all played our part. We've all proved ourselves a little too eager to rush out and buy what they're selling. We are the ones who stand in line to buy an iPhone. We are the ones who see the Alexa commercials and run to Amazon.com to order one. Nobody is blameless here, including me. I've got an iPhone. As I think I noted during the pancake discussion, I look at it a lot.

On some level, everyone from the very top of our society to the very bottom has bought stock in the idea that technology will deliver a better future than the one we're heading for. It always has. At least it always has when you look at history as history—the 30,000-foot view. Time heals wounds. Distance provides perspective. But if you take a more granular view and look at history as a set of real things that happen to real people in real time, well, it becomes easier to see that the future hasn't always been kind to everyone. For some, the better future that technology promised turned out to be a human catastrophe. But we'll get to that.

The conspirators I mentioned—including you and me—view it as an inevitability that the time will come when artificial intelligence and the Internet of Things are the primary tools we use to navigate the world around us. Insomuch as you or someone you know is in a position to profit from its arrival, the Internet of Things may strike you as a glorious inevitability. It's coming, they tell us, so we might as well get used to it. One day soon we all will live in an easy paradise of not just smartphones and smart cars but smart houses and smart refrigerators: our every need anticipated and satisfied; our every instinct cataloged, analyzed, and systematized for our benefit and for the benefit of all mankind. Big data has big dreams.

"Dream big," wasn't that Apple's slogan for a while?

We're already more than halfway to that easy paradise. "Smart machines now collect our highway tolls, check us out at stores, take our blood pressure, massage our backs, give us directions, answer our phones, print our documents, transmit our messages, rock our babies, read our books, turn on our lights, shine our shoes, guard our homes, fly our planes, write our wills, teach our children, kill our enemies, and the list goes on," wrote economists Jeffrey Sachs and Laurence Kotlikoff in a 2012 working paper for the National Bureau of Economic Research. It's all for our comfort. Who doesn't want to live in a world where the fridge knows when you're out of beer and orders you an icy cold six-pack of your favorite hoppy IPA, at a great price, one better than any store in your neighborhood can offer, and then delivers it directly to your front door—by drone—within an hour?

The short answer is: me. I don't want to live in that world. Why? Because I understand the tradeoffs. Icy cold beer is something I support. Flying through a tollbooth with my E-ZPass certainly beats waiting in a long line of traffic with the kids squirming and screeching in the back seat. I'm fine with e-mail, texting, and video chat. I use these things all the time and get a lot out of them. What concerns me is what I must give up to get these conveniences. I worry that the price will be a little more than any of us bargained for when we said, "Sure, I think I would like to have my music, pictures, books, and newspapers, a street-by-street map of the world, a clock, a flashlight, my address book, an e-mail account, an instant-messaging service, the Internet, and a calculator all rolled up into one handsome device that fits in my pocket but can also order a taxi and adjust the temperature in my home."

I didn't sign up for the Internet of Things. Did you? I don't think you did, and that's what I mean by a conspiracy—the water is so nice and so warm that we frogs don't realize it's starting to boil. Well, maybe some of us do, but only when it's too late to do anything about it. That's how a conspiracy works; you keep the secret until you can't keep it any longer. Then, immediately pivot and present it as a fait accompli. "It's too late to turn back," the conspirators will say. "We've come too far." And we dupes buy in because we like the toys.

That, my friend, is how you ram the future down people's throats, one big dream at a time.

A great many people my age harbor extreme anxiety about this wired-up digital future. Many of our millennial cousins—not to mention tech boosters, futurists, journalists, tastemakers, and the naively optimistic—tend to view anyone with more than a dollop of doubt about this slowly gestating *Star Trek* world as reactionaries, or worse. The preferred term is "Luddite." The word is hurled about with alarming frequency and with political malice aforethought. It's meant to slander the questioners, the skeptics, the concerned, or the merely unconvinced as rubes who are as afraid of technology and progress as they are of their own shadows. Luddites are always and everywhere on the "wrong side of history." If the Luddites had had their way, we'd all be living in small communities, working with primitive tools to eke out a subsistence existence. The Luddites had little dreams, not big ones. Because of their provincialism and shortsightedness, they missed the boat.

That's the rap, anyway. But it's a bad rap. What is a Luddite, really? Let's take a moment to look at where the word comes from and why it has become such a recognizable epithet.

The term first appeared in the British Midlands during the early 19th century. Weavers, combers, croppers, finishers, dressers of wool, framework knitters, stockingers, and lace-workers had managed to find a subsistence-level niche as suppliers and intermediate producers in the trade at the heart of the British textile economy. The original Luddites recognized that the Industrial Revolution then sweeping the British Isles represented an existential threat to their village way of life. They weren't wrong. The coal-fired, steam-powered, multistory mills then springing up on the valley floors across the counties of Cheshire, Derbyshire, Lancashire, Nottinghamshire, and Yorkshire were visibly and inarguably robbing these petty artisans and traditional craftsmen of their livelihoods, the only livelihoods they had ever known or were likely to know absent a willingness to give themselves over to six-and-a-half-day weeks of pure, laborious monotony working for the local mill owner. Not surprisingly, some found this prospect unappealing.

In their hundreds, if not their thousands, textile workers in the towns and villages across central England formed small militias and raiding parties. Under cover of night they began attacking the hulking and impersonal mills, smashing windows and destroying—or attempting to—the steam-powered looms and other machinery contained within. They carried carbines, pistols, pikes, hammers, and in some cases large rocks. Often they met resistance in the form of local constables or private guards enlisted by the mill owner to protect his investment.

The movement took as its inspiration a mythical character named General Ned Ludd, himself supposedly a weaver who rose up against the creeping mechanization of the textile industry a few years prior to the full-blown Luddite insurrection of 1812. Luddism blossomed in a part of England already known for an earlier, possibly apocryphal purveyor of vigilante justice—Robin Hood. As with the Merry Men, the Luddites' activities inspired a brutal reprisal. The British government, in tight alliance with the capitalist class and the landed aristocracy, put its shoulder into the job of smashing the Luddite movement. And smash it they did. Clashes between the Luddite militias and the mill owners' hired guns were brief but bloody. Many men died, and those who didn't became targets of a vengeful state. They were hunted like bandits, sentenced to death, and publicly hanged—in one instance, 14 Luddites were executed at the same time.

Luddism was more than simply an instinctual lashing out against technological progress. It was a righteous crusade, with enough interior logic and external coherence to inspire thousands of regular people to take up arms against injustice. That's no easy thing to do in a settled society like the U.K. in the early 19th century. "The real challenge of the Luddites was not so much the physical one, against the machines and manufacturers, but a moral one, calling into question on the grounds of justice and fairness the underlying assumptions of the [new] political economy," wrote the left-wing journalist Kirkpatrick Sale in his 1995 history of the Luddite movement, *Rebels against the Future*. The Luddites struck a chord, and for a lot of people it sounded not like social justice but like the real kind.

The Industrial Revolution in England was a shocking thing. It uprooted lives, transformed the landscape, despoiled the environment, and changed forever Britain's national culture. Of course, many will argue that the Industrial Revolution was not only necessary but a massive success in the aggregate, so even if the Luddites had a sympathetic political point to make in the short term, it can't be defended given what we know now. Two centuries gone, the Luddites look to have made a terribly bad bet on what industrialization would do for the world. The efficiencies gained by the mechanization of labor and the specialization that this allowed improved output, satisfied demand for British products—maybe even created greater demand—and ultimately increased prosperity across the board, not only in England and the United Kingdom but, as the principles of market capitalism and openness to trade spread around the globe, in the far corners of the earth as well.

All of this is true and cannot be contradicted; capitalism's poverty-slaying powers are not in doubt. The Industrial Revolution kicked off 200 years of practically straight-line economic growth. The forces it unleashed have lifted people out of the desperate, grinding, intergenerational misery that had been their lot. People's lives are materially better than they would have been because of the Industrial Revolution. But to sit back and suggest that it was all good, or merely a necessary period of creative destruction in the economy, is implicitly to sanction all manner of barbarity and conquest in the name of progress—political, technological, or otherwise. You won't catch me doing it.

We all know the famous John Maynard Keynes quotation: "In the long run, we'll all be dead." Economic theories that appeal to long-term benefit—meaning we'll need to wait more than a generation or two to see how great things will turn out—are never going to convince ordinary people in the here and now. They will always need to be imposed through force or trickery. People are smart enough to know that some nice-sounding reforms to help everyone get a bigger piece of a bigger pie in the long run are going to screw them personally good and hard in the short run.

When I read the history of the Luddite rebellion, my sympathies are not with the mill owners and the British government. On the contrary, my heart goes out to the people who were robbed of their entire means and manner of living. The dislocation was real, as were the people who were dislocated, though they can seem remote—even a joke—from our distant perch here in the 21st century. The suffering and anxiety experienced by the Luddites were not imaginary. The people who took up arms against the steam-powered loom were not irrational. It's easy to caricature them as dumb, shortsighted, or selfish, but they had a point—a good point, and they deserve not to have their names slandered across history.

More, their point still stands. Luddism, writes Kirkpatrick Sale, "is a strain of opposition, of naysaying, that has not been dispelled in all these decades by however many elaborate machines or more elaborate visions the technophiles have paraded." The Luddites sought to preserve a status quo that worked for them. They understood it and wanted to pass it on to their children. In our modern culture, we don't have much patience for the status quo. Everything is a problem. There are enough historical wrongs that need to be righted that the average person becomes convinced that nothing, no bit of the past, has ever been good. Nothing has ever been true. No one who wants to preserve the status quo could possibly be anything other than selfish, stupid, scared, or extremely shortsighted.

We love the long view. In the early 21st century, no figure in the public imagination receives more approbation than the "visionary," the man or woman who can see past the miserable status quo to a new way of living—presumably a better one—in which yesterday's hard problems are solved so easily and so quickly that it becomes possible to believe that they were never actually problems in the first place, just shortcomings of imagination. Life is lived in the short term, yet "visionaries" are so called because they look beyond the short term to a world transformed. Too often these days we lionize anyone with the mere ability to imagine a different future. How often do we stop to ask whether it's a good future? Not often enough for my tastes.

It's notable the degree to which I agree with Sale's assessment of, and sympathy for, the aims of the Luddite movement, considering that we come at the question from different angles. Sale views the Industrial Revolution and its attendant disruptions as a capitalist plot to break up poor communities and put them to work in service of the ownership class's greed. It's the classic case of profit over people—the imperatives of business demands that the peasantry must be separated from their simplistic, traditional ways of doing things, and turned into cogs in the great manufacturing machine. It has a Marxist logic: all a man has to sell is his labor, and if you divorce him from that, you break his spirit. If you break a man's spirit, he will not resist when you rob him of his community attachments and family ties. Never mind all that. All that matters is that the shareholders profit.

I am no Marxist. If you have read this far, you should be fairly convinced that I am an American conservative in the Ronald Reagan mode. I am the sort of fellow whose first instinct is always to resist social change. But for Britain's Industrial Revolution to succeed, the old ways clearly had to be smashed. From the vantage point of history, it may seem an inevitability—even a glorious one. From the point of view of the croppers and artisans living in the counties of Cheshire, Derbyshire, Lancashire, Nottinghamshire, and Yorkshire, the Industrial Revolution was an unambiguous catastrophe. It doesn't take a Marxist to see that.

Luddism wasn't so much a rebellion against technological progress as it was a well-placed kick against a belief in the saving power of technology. Principally, the Luddites were upset that they hadn't been consulted. Their old-fashioned, simplistic views were deemed immaterial; their traditions and preferences inconsequential; their voices and concerns meaningless. They were told in so many words to get with the changing program, because the program was going forward whether they liked it or not. These days, reaction against such thinking smells less like Sale's modern progressivism and more like my conservatism.

Today's Luddite, like a 21st-century William F. Buckley, Jr., stands athwart the Internet of Things yelling "Stop!"

* * *

If the artificial-intelligence agenda is a soft conspiracy to come between us and the human-scaled world that we've known and loved, the question remains: why? Why does Silicon Valley go to all this trouble to develop and sell us these incrementally interconnected gizmos and gadgets? Why do they seek to divorce us from the habits and activities that have defined our lives, things like driving, shopping, and—we'll get to this—working. What's in it for them? Two things spring to mind: financial profit and social control. Explaining the financial profit side of the story is easy. The social control side of the story will take a little longer to tease out.

Everybody on some level seeks wealth—to live better, to help others, or just to play with more and cooler toys. We find wealth attractive. We lust after it. We are a greedy species, though it must be said that we come by the impulse naturally. Evolution has programmed *Homo sapiens* to take as much stuff as we can get, when we can get it, and for as long as we can get it, because we know deep down that the chance might not come again, or it might not come again soon. So on one level Silicon Valley tech titans are no different than the rest of us. Maybe a little more motivated than the average guy to find ways to get rich. Maybe a little more tolerant of risk. At root, though, they are just wealth-pursuing, profit-maximizing ladies and gentlemen—*Homo economicus.*

On another level, they aren't a bit like us. They fancy themselves the vanguard, visionaries who see farther and better than the rest of us. They are more productive and more imaginative than 100 of us put together. Their hubris leads them to try to impose a new future on the world. They do it not by force but by infiltration, by slowly—persistently—insinuating their products into our lives. These products are attractive; they are status symbols, they are time-savers; they make things easier; but they are slowly transforming society from one in which the individual has a reasonable expectation of physical privacy and personal agency into one in which the individual voluntarily exchanges his privacy and agency for ever-greater degrees of ease and comfort. A spoonful of sugar helps the social control go down.

Technology critic Nicholas Carr has termed the tech-obsessed visionaries "starry-eyed futurists" who, "[b]y spreading a utopian view of technology, a view that defines progress as essentially technological, they've encouraged people to switch off their critical faculties and give Silicon Valley entrepreneurs and financiers free rein in remaking culture to fit their commercial interests." In a 2016 collection of essays called *Utopia Is Creepy*—his follow-up to *The Shallows*—Carr hammers the "culture of distraction and dependency" that the great, saving, interconnected technology of the web has brought us. Kirkpatrick Sale calls skeptics like me and Carr "neo-Luddites." He means it as a compliment (at least I think he does). We share a deep suspicion that trading privacy for comfort will ultimately prove very far from worth the cost. "Where the neo-Luddites may be found, they are attempting to bear witness to the secret little truth that lies at the heart of the modern experience," Sale writes. "[W]hatever its presumed benefits, of speed or ease or power or wealth, industrial technology comes at a price, and in the contemporary world that price is ever rising and ever threatening."

The price of technological ease and comfort, in my view, is paid in the one commodity of which each of us is allotted a fixed amount, and no more: time. Minutes spent scrolling your Twitter feed or curating your Instagram are minutes you don't get back. Hours spent playing Minecraft or Jewel Mania are hours you might as well lop off the end of your life. Days spent tied to the Internet of Things are days spent in bondage to a future you won't control.

NINE

Money for Nothing

What is the vision of the future that Silicon Valley has in mind and that millennials are so eager to embrace? It's not the one you probably imagined for yourself when you were a teenager, unless you happened to have grown up with a particular dream of living out your adult years on the starship *Enterprise*. Come to think of it, the self-sustaining, self-explaining world of *Star Trek* isn't the worst analogy for the all-encompassing tech future at which our Silicon Valley overlords are aiming. On the *Enterprise*, a handful of superbly qualified specialists assigned themselves the lion's share of responsibility for running the ship, carrying out the prime directive, and boldly going where no man had gone before. To viewers, the *Enterprise* seemed like a rather large vessel, but almost everyone apart from the show's stars existed out of sight. You didn't see much of them, unless they became a necessary plot device.

What was everyone else on the ship doing while Captain Kirk, Mr. Spock, Bones, Scotty, Chekov, Sulu, and Uhura were getting into and out of interstellar scrapes? Who knows, but they weren't making nearly the contribution to the ship's ongoing mission as the better-looking, more heroic bigshots were. They formed a kind of disposable service class rarely seen or heard from, rarely even noticed by the officers on the bridge. The most productive members of this particular society carried the drama forward. Everyone else was a bit player.

Of course, the coolest part about *Star Trek* was the omniscient, disembodied voice known as "computer" that could be called on anywhere at any time to answer any question. It wasn't just an eerily prescient blueprint for the Internet. It *was* that; but it was more. It was artificial intelligence with the capability of doing complex—and sometimes abstract—computation on the fly. It had the ability to engage in hypotheticals and had a physical dimension as well. It was not just the ship's brain; it was the ship itself. It could execute. In its conception and presentation, the *Enterprise*'s computer was close to what *WIRED* magazine founder Kevin Kelly has called "the technium"—a discrete "superorganism of computation."

Kelly has posited the emergence of a global cloud, a computer of computers above and apart from any one advanced technology. The technium is a *summa* of the world's computing power: all of its desktops, laptops, mainframes, servers, cell phones, tablets, and landlines rolled into one. Throw in the cars and the ovens and the baby monitors and the wireless printers from the Internet of Things, too. Sometimes Kelly calls it the One Machine, the sum total of all the hardware and software working, humming, and resonating in an ever-closer harmony of artificial intelligence. "It has its own force that exerts," Kelly has said. "That force is part cultural (influenced by and influencing of humans), but it's also partly non-human, partly indigenous to the physics of technology itself. That's the part that is scary and interesting." I'm not sure what's interesting about it, but I must say I do see the scary bits.

The visionary "geniuses" of Silicon Valley seem at best totally ambivalent about the idea of calling such a technium into being. At worst, they are so eager for it they can barely contain themselves. Call it delusions of grandeur, call it the God complex, or call it plain old ordinary lust for power, but the most well-respected entrepreneurs— the celebrated "visionaries" of tech—all have one thing in common: they think they know better than the rest of us how society should run. Basically they envision a pyramid-shaped political economy, with themselves and the superproductive Silicon Valley workforce at the top and the rest of us plebes spanning out below in a massive, obedient, and grateful base. The bad news is they have the means to try to make this happen, and the implicit support of the soon-to-be governed, which derives from a record of a decade or more of supplying everyone with the coolest toys—the things we didn't know we wanted until we got them.

Steve Jobs, the Google guys—Larry Page and Sergey Brin—Bill Gates, Jeff Bezos, Mark Zuckerberg, Peter Thiel, Elon Musk—these are the crew I refer to as the "techdaddies." If they desire social control, it's only because they love us so much. These guys just know that the technium, when it matures into its full potential, is going to be great for everyone. But it will benefit them most of all, because it will give them—and their smart, talented, productive ilk—a place of undeniable privilege at the top of that pyramid. Why shouldn't it be thus? They've already proved their worth.

The techdaddies also know that wacky ideas sometimes become reality. In the Dream Big world of Silicon Valley, this has translated into an attitude of "the wackier the better." If you can dream it, it can be done. The list of Google's wacky ideas is too long to print here, or maybe to print anywhere, but they range from the achievable—scanning every book that's ever been published—to the silly—a "space elevator" connected to an orbiting satellite. In the near future expect Google to offer you the computing power and Internet connectivity of a smartphone in the form of a contact lens or the windshield of a self-driving car. Captain Kirk would be envious.

Google's futurists have also bandied about impossible dreams that they call "moonshots," wildest-imagination stuff such as mining asteroids for rare minerals. In the end, however, those projects are just small beer. In 2013, Google launched the California Life Company, or Calico, a mysterious "longevity lab" whose goal is to extend human life spans. The venture prompted *TIME* magazine to ask in a headline, "Can Google Solve Death?" Maybe I'm crazy, but I sort of doubt it. For one thing, if they did manage to pull it off, it would create something of an overcrowding problem. I suppose Google thinks they can fix that, too.

Facebook's boy genius Mark Zuckerberg's big dream—apart from maybe one day becoming president of the United States—is to engineer a way for us to send our innermost thoughts directly to each other's minds via instant-message telepathy. Call it thought mail. "One day, I believe we'll be able to send full, rich thoughts to each other directly using technology," he said during a 2015 question-and-answer session. "You'll just be able to think of something and your friends will immediately be able to experience it, too, if you'd like." This idea is no doubt born of a charitable impulse to assist those who cannot speak for one reason or another, or to eliminate the problem of texting while driving, but it is nonetheless supremely misguided.

Actually, I'm being too polite. It's the stupidest thing I've ever heard.

I can think of few things I desire less than to have other people's thoughts—complete with emojis and a soundtrack?—beamed into my head as I'm trying to go about my business. The plan has pitfalls for sender and receiver alike. As Nicholas Carr quips, "That's really going to require some incredible impulse control." Then again, maybe it won't, since many of us have already given up on ever being able to control ourselves around technology anyway.

Above my personal desires not to be constantly bothered by incoming thought mail is a more urgent concern. As we have learned from the hacking, data dumps, privacy breaches, and security failures of recent years, nothing on the Internet—or connected to the Internet—is private. Or, if it is, it won't be for long. The Internet and everything wired into it is public, or potentially public. That means your e-mails, online purchases, reading habits, and social media comments will all eventually become easy fodder for the Peeping Toms and digital historians of the future. Connecting your home, office, and car to the Internet means anything that happens inside those formerly private spaces is similarly at risk of exposure to the wider world. Inviting a technology company into your living room is bad enough, but inviting one into your mind? You'd have to be crazy.

If you're a Silicon Valley techdaddy, however, maybe nothing is too crazy to contemplate. "This plan is so crazy, it just might work" was a classic plot convention of late-boomer, early Gen-X television culture, and the tech visionaries seem to have fully digested it. Jeff Bezos had the idea to start Amazon while driving alone across the country. He was evidently inspired by all those hours spent in blissful solitary contemplation, because one of the wildest-dream projects he supports with his vast fortune is the 10,000 Year Clock. A 200-foot-tall timekeeper built into the side of a mountain in West Texas, the clock has so far cost the multibillionaire north of $40 million. Why is he doing it? As Bezos told the *Wall Street Journal* in 2012: "The reason I'm doing it is that it is a symbol of long-term thinking.... We humans have become so technologically sophisticated that in certain ways we're dangerous to ourselves. It's going to be increasingly important over time for humanity to take a longer-term view of its future."

Say what now?

This fellow, Bezos, who has made several fortunes of unfathomable dimension by selling the world a technologically sophisticated lifestyle of spiritual ease, material comfort, and high-touch customer service, now turns tail and warns that technological sophistication makes us…dangerous? One can be forgiven for wanting to know to whom or to what. Don't you think it's a wee bit rich that a guy who never saw an industry he didn't want to disrupt should have the—what should we call it?—*nerve* to tell us that we've gone too far? I hate to say it, but if we've gone too far, Amazon and its ilk bear the lion's share of the blame. What we're becoming may be dangerous—I tend to think it is—but a lot of it was your doing, Jeff.

Peter Thiel and Elon Musk founded the payment service PayPal to help facilitate commercial transactions online. Thiel has gone on to found several other highly successful firms, including Palantir Technologies, which uses Big Data to help governments do anti-terror and anti-crime work, among other things. Musk has used his billions to seed a range of companies with moonshots in mind. Tesla Inc. makes $90,000 electric cars and gigantic batteries (all of which are highly subsidized by taxpayers). SpaceX is a private outer-space exploration firm that would love to give you a ride to Mars someday. Musk's Boring Company is trying to persuade state and local governments to let him dig tunnels throughout the U.S. so that another of his companies, Hyperloop, can solve the country's traffic problems.

Both Thiel and Musk have decided that mankind, in order to save itself, needs to find new ways of living—including, even, new environments in which to live. Musk thinks we ought to colonize other planets. Thiel famously invested in the Seasteading Institute, which sought to create sustainable floating cities on the vast oceans covering most of the earth. Though he has lately backed away from his dreams of a waterworld, Thiel has expressed other controversial beliefs, notably about the compatibility of freedom and democracy: "Because there are no truly free places left in our world, I suspect that the mode for escape must involve some sort of new and hitherto untried process that leads us to some undiscovered country; and for this reason I have focused my efforts on new technologies that may create a new space for freedom."

Thiel is a libertarian, and his view of freedom is as elegant in theory as all libertarian philosophy. In close contact with harsh reality, however, the theory almost always falls apart like wet paper. Thiel seeks to invent a new, less harsh reality that better aligns with the beauty and elegance of his theory. Do you doubt that his attempts to usher in a brave new world will end in technological totalitarianism? From the pages of fiction to the pages of history, all brave new worlds do.

Silicon Valley's billionaire CEOs are aware that their disruptive passions will likely unleash reactionary social forces beyond their ability to control. In fact, the technium that they themselves are gleefully and profitably calling into being may amplify and extend that reaction, pushing it deeper and farther than it would ever have gone under its own steam. Is it possible that the blowback could go so far, so fast that it threatens to bring a premature halt to the wackiest of the techdaddies' moonshots?

That would be something. But these are smart guys, renowned for their talent for seeing over hills and around corners. They're not stumbling blindly forward into this potentially chaotic future without a plan. They know perfectly well that their gadgets, apps, self-driving cars, thought-reading devices, brain-mail programs, back-flipping robots, algorithm ads, surveillance toys, space elevators, floating cities, outer-space colonies, and all the rest will push humanity into an ever more complete reliance on "smart machines" to do the kinds of low- or no-skill jobs that once provided satisfying livelihoods to millions of people. One by one the lower rungs of the economic and employment ladders will be lopped off by high-performance cyborgs that can cook and serve a meal, clean a house, fix a car, or teach a child to read at almost no marginal cost. That's going to upset more than a few apple carts. The techdaddies know it. They know, too, that not everybody is cut out to be a Google engineer or a Facebook programmer—or even an Apple store Genius Bar service professional.

The Silicon Valley economy, as incredibly productive as it is and will continue to be, won't be able to provide a job for every American who wants one. By vaporizing demand for low-skilled labor and putting hundreds of thousands of Americans out of work, Silicon Valley's big brains will find themselves staring down the barrel of some serious social unrest. It's not unreasonable to expect economic upheaval and possibly even revolution.

Naturally, visionaries that they are, the techdaddies have already settled upon a remedy: the universal basic income, a guaranteed minimum welfare payment to everyone in the country regardless of income level, ability to work, or employment status. "A lot of exciting new innovations are going to be created, which will generate a lot of opportunities and wealth, but there is a real danger it could also reduce the amount of jobs," wrote billionaire Virgin CEO Richard Branson in an August 2017 blog post. "This will make experimenting with ideas like basic income even more important in the years to come."

The idea is simple: removing the need to fend for yourself in the cutthroat economy of the technium will free you up to pursue your secret dreams of writing a novel, staying home with your kids, or starting that online business for which you could never quite find the time. The universal basic income will ensure that you never find yourself worrying about paying for, well, the basics. Food, clothing, and shelter will be well within your reach. Beyond that, how you choose to pursue happiness will be up to you.

"We should make it so that no one is worried about how they're going to pay for a place to live, no one has to worry about how they're going to have enough to eat," says Sam Altman, president of Y Combinator, the influential Mountain View, California, "accelerator" fund that invests in tech startups. "Just give people enough money to have a reasonable quality of life." It's a nice theory, if a little paternalistic.[8] But there are a couple of obvious flaws. First, do we all agree on what level of income constitutes a "reasonable quality of life?" I have a hard time believing that we do. Someone, somewhere is going to grant themselves the power to decide what that level is. I have a feeling it will be someone with a proven talent for seeing around corners.

Here's another problem: the techdaddies think that you won't mind losing your old livelihood, since it was probably pretty unfulfilling work to begin with and you probably hated pulling your tired, undereducated carcass out of bed in the morning only to be insulted all day by your junior college-trained business-major boss[9] who insisted on looking over

---

8 What did you expect from your techdaddies?
9 He is going to lose his livelihood, too.

your shoulder while you performed meaningless, mindless, manual labor for just a few bucks more than minimum wage.

That's what they think. If for some strange reason it turns out you actually found satisfaction in providing for yourself and your family by driving a cab or working at the widget factory or waiting tables or cleaning motel rooms, they think you'll be willing to accept the basic-income payoff as compensation for the disruption to your livelihood. It's a win-win, they think. You get some free money and they don't need to worry about you and your old pals from the shop floor, the motel, the cab service, the auto shop, or the trucking company coming after them with torches and pitchforks.

The universal basic income is a bribe, plain and simple. Are you ready to have your palm greased?

Silicon Valley's biggest names have lined up behind the idea of a universal basic income. Musk says "it's going to be necessary." Tim Berners-Lee, inventor of the World Wide Web, views it as a tool for combating income inequality. Bill Gates says we're not ready for it yet, but promises that the day is shortly coming when we will be. Mark Zuckerberg thinks of it as a "cushion" that allows you to "try new things."

After returning from a 2017 campaign-style trip to Alaska, a state that pays every resident an annual average oil-income dividend of $1,000, Zuckerberg said: "When you're losing money, your mentality is largely about survival. But when you're profitable, you're confident about your future and you look for opportunities to invest and grow further. Alaska's economy has historically created this winning mentality, which has led to this basic income." One of the selling points that Zuckerberg and his peers have seized on is that universal basic income is an idea that supposedly transcends the liberal/conservative ideological trap. It may seem on its face like a dream cooked up in the big-government liberal kitchen, but universal basic income actually has roots in conservative economics.

Towering Austrian school economists like Freidrich Hayek and Milton Friedman supported the idea of what they called a "negative income tax," under which anyone making below a certain annual income receives a cash payment from the government at tax time rather than the other way around. The conservative intellectual Charles Murray has also endorsed the idea of a $10,000 annual payment to everyone over 21 years old. The Friedman approach, which lives today in the American tax code as the Earned Income Tax Credit for families with children, has the benefit of incentivizing work. The amount of the credit rises with each dollar of earned income. But often left out of the story are Friedman and Murray's caveats, the prime one being that any guaranteed income program should be offered in lieu of other welfare programs, not in addition to them.

"The proposal for a negative income tax is a proposal to help poor people by giving them money, which is what they need," Friedman told William F. Buckley, Jr., on a 1968 episode of *Firing Line*. "Rather than, as now, by requiring them to come before a governmental official, detail all their assets and their liabilities, and be told that you may spend X dollars on rent, Y dollars on food, et cetera, and then be given a handout." When the techdaddies extol the "bipartisan" nature of the universal basic income idea, it's not clear they fully appreciate that they're allying themselves with free-market conservatives who seek to dismantle the infrastructure of the welfare state that liberal Democrats have spent the past 80 years diligently constructing.

Many on the left have an entirely different view of the purpose and utility of the universal basic income. To them it seems like just one more government safety-net program on the road to what they like to call Democratic socialism. That's the happy kind of socialism, the one you find in much of Western Europe, where a handful of national-champion businesses produce geysers of cash that the state then redistributes to the less productive, less well-endowed, and less educated members of society. Democratic socialism is the capitalist alternative where nobody can ever be fired, so nobody ever gets hired. Bill Gross, founder of the trillion-dollar Newport Beach–based investment firm PIMCO, says that if a universal basic income "strikes you as a form of socialism, I would suggest we get used to it."

There's a reason why Silicon Valley—not Paris, Frankfurt, Stockholm, or Milan—is and always will be the hot center of tech innovation. Maybe it never occurs to the techdaddies that the industry their ingenuity has built, and the titanic wealth and prosperity they've personally enjoyed as a result of succeeding in that industry, has really only ever been historically possible in a country like the United States, where a vibrant private economy is governed by relatively light regulation and low-ish taxes, robust property-rights protections and the rule of law, and an entrepreneurial culture that rewards risk-taking. Are they under the impression that Silicon Valley is the last industry the world will ever know or need, so we can safely shut down the 250-year American experiment in ordered liberty and limited government? That's Bond villain–level hubris, which, to be honest, some of these guys have been flirting with for a while.

There are other, more practical issues to consider before signing over America's economic future to the universal basic income. "Basic income sounds to many like an attractive idea—but closer examination reveals that it's also a dangerous one, based on dubious social and moral logic," concludes the urbanist Aaron Renn, who rightly points out that such a program would require far more restrictive immigration controls than many on the left would ever probably be comfortable with. Basic income boosters, writes Renn, frequently gloss over the thornier ethical issues to which the idea gives rise. In a review for *City Journal* of a book by Philippe Van Parijs and Yannick Vanderborght called *Basic Income: A Radical Proposal for a Free Society and a Sane Economy*, Renn excoriates the authors' "intrinsic vision" as "morally problematic, even perverse." It's a vision of society in which "individuals are entitled to a share of social prosperity but have no obligation to contribute anything to it."

What Renn doesn't say—but I will—is that this is and always has been the ethic governing almost every Silicon Valley innovation. "Information wants to be free," partisans of the early Internet used to insist. From Napster to YouTube, the digital ethos has been to fling open the gates and invite all comers; to drive established industries into the proverbial ditch by offering the products they once sold at no cost—or below cost; to undermine America's bourgeois values and hollow out its mediating institutions; to boldly go where no man has gone before.

There's a reason that Silicon Valley eggheads call themselves futurists. To the techdaddies and their followers, the past is a dead letter, a broiling slowpoke, a vast wasteland of ugly ideas, simple machines, hot wars, and petty political squabbles. Nothing much truly creative ever happened there until Bill Gates and Paul Allen founded Microsoft. The world had little purpose, and almost no beauty, until Steve Jobs and Jony Ive gave it the iPhone.

In part, this relentless focus on the glorious future derives from the entrepreneurial culture of risk that permeates Silicon Valley, where past failures are merely prerequisites for future success. But it also derives from the paradox that all successful people must grapple with—am I successful because I'm superior, or am I superior because I'm successful? Almost all of the techdaddies appear to have concluded that their own superiority is what drove their success. Perhaps the most successful moneymakers of every age similarly succumb to the hubris of self-celebration. But unlike yesteryear's robber barons, the techdaddies have achieved almost unimaginable levels of wealth and success at alarmingly young ages—some of them are in their late thirties or early forties and have been billionaires since their mid-twenties. Their success has given them the means to remake society; their sense of superiority has given them the inherent right to do so; and their youth has given them the time.

Buckle your seat belts. It's going to be a bumpy few decades.

TEN

Right Here, Right Now

The term "slacker" always struck me as funny—it still does. I had no idea when I first heard it in 1985 that in just a few years it would adhere to my generation like a tattoo. Some of us wore it as a badge of honor. It meant we were a new entry in the long story of 20th-century American generational "types." Like flappers, preppies, beats, greasers, folkies, hippies, punks, new wavers, valley girls, and nerds, slackers were an identifiable thing—a little ambitionless, clad in thrift-store clothing, ironically defiant, and likely listening either to the first generation of mainstream hip-hop artists or to the new breed of guitar-heavy rock music being made in and around Seattle. A slacker was an early-'90s kid who didn't quite have a plan, but who sort of liked reading magazines, knew a little bit about a lot of things, maybe took five years to finish college, and probably wasn't going to hurt anyone even if making a bazillion dollars wasn't in the cards.

We weren't just jocks or punks or burnouts, or even the little brothers and little sisters of jocks, punks, and burnouts. We were ourselves alone. The rebellion wasn't without cause. It had a genus and species.

In 1991, the year I graduated from high school, a new movie showed up on the shelves of the same video store where I'd once rented *Back to the Future*. The term "independent film" hadn't yet seeped into the broader culture, but Richard Linklater's *Slacker* was the prototypical indie. It was meandering, atmospheric, and weird, and whatever was going on with the characters didn't quite add up to a plot. It was a series of interconnected conversations between unknown actors, some of whom seemed to be amateurs, playing sketchily drawn parts. Two people would be engaged in a philosophical discussion about this or that seemingly unimportant thing, and the exchange would ultimately lead nowhere in particular. When the camera had had enough of one conversation, it would catch on like a hitchhiker with another conversation and ride with it for a while. The whole thing was low-budget, weird, very much of its time and place, and mildly exciting for a pretentious 18-year-old film fan looking for something a little richer than *Back to the Future II…or III.*

I found myself exploring the world that produced movies like *Slacker*, which, pretentious though they may have been, were fundamentally sincere and took their time to do something creative and unique, to distance themselves from the usual stale Hollywood offerings. I wasn't the only one who thought so—the American independent cinema phenomenon was picking up steam and would soon become a force.

I grew my hair long and started wearing flannel shirts and Dr. Martens boots. I wasn't the only one who did that, either. To be a slacker was to care more about things like music, art, and books than about things like college, relationship, and career. That was me from about 1992 to 1996. I had no ambition to find meaningful work, or to line up my life in a neat row of goals and accomplishments. I just wanted enough money to be able to see a few movies and buy my own records.

I should be honest: part of me still wants that.

But if I didn't have money, career, or an all-consuming ambition in those days, I also didn't have an iPhone in my pocket feeding me nonstop pictorial updates from friends and relatives who did have those things. I knew a few people then with good jobs. Some were in promising relationships, their lives advancing in a rational progression. I may have at times been a little jealous of how well they seemed to be doing, but I wasn't torturing myself with constant comparison via social media. In order to peek at their lives I had to scrape myself off the couch and deliver myself to school or work or my parents' house or the record store or the dive bar or the music club—or any of the other places where human beings congregated to share information, tell stories about themselves, make career connections, show off their new tattoos, and find love.[10] Barring that, I had to send my friends postcards and letters to find out what they were up to. Even if I wasn't particularly motivated to launch my adulthood, I also wasn't sitting on the couch, stewing in the suspicion that I was falling behind my peers in the race of life.

Millennials, on the other hand, report high levels of anxiety and depression due to the constant pressure of keeping up appearances on social media. Did you just get dumped or lose your job? Well, too bad. I'm sorry to say that your college friends are all getting married and getting promoted and they'll be posting updates daily just to remind you how crummy your life has become.

The millennial social-media landscape is a brand new thing—a highly competitive and meticulously curated wire service pumping out a steady stream of well-produced personal updates and career milestones from everyone you've ever met. It's created a generation that is at once narcissistic and insecure, predisposed to boasting and secretly resentful of others' good fortune. It's a weird mix. It can't be good for the mental health of the nation.

As I have noted here repeatedly, the pace of technological change is quickening. The rate of extinction of human-scale products and behaviors that Americans of all ages once took for granted, like magazines, jalopies, dating, and face-to-face conversation, is also accelerating at an accelerating rate. When was the last time you sat on a park bench and watched the world go by without looking at your smartphone? When was the last time you spent a morning with your kids without wondering what was happening on Facebook, Instagram, Snapchat, or Twitter? When was the last time you browsed the racks at a book or record store? When was the last time you listened to a whole record, wrote a real letter, or read a book without peeking at your phone every 90 seconds? When was the last time you sat down and read the entire newspaper instead of just scanning the headlines? When was the last time you saw a play? When was the last time you went to a ball game?

For me, I can honestly say, it has been a long time on most of these fronts. The nature of my job is such that I must keep an eye on politics and current events, but the cold truth of it is I check in on Twitter and

---

10 It was hard to get out of the 1990s without a tattoo.

Facebook way more often than I should. Am I addicted? I don't honestly know. But I don't like what I feel myself becoming, and I suspect that many of my generation feel the same way. Given the eager technological acquiescence of the digital natives, the members of Generation X have an awesome responsibility to keep faith with reality. And by "reality," I mean the nondigital world. If we don't do it, who will?

The analog world that shaped us is fading from memory. We can't turn back time, or turn the technology train around, but we can slow it down. We can give this revolutionary moment context, and ensure that the transformation we are undergoing proceeds in the most thoughtful and productive way possible. It ought to be within our reach to enjoy incremental technological advances and improvements without buying into the Silicon Valley dreamworld of digital currencies, driverless cars, thought mail, sex robots, drone deliveries, smart houses, and universal basic income. Do we really need to restock our refrigerators without ever seeing another person? Is it really a good idea to let a big corporation know everything about you, from your personal predilections and preferences to your genetic profile and medical history? Do you really need a phone that can only be unlocked by scanning your face?

For me, the answer is "no." As the still-building millennial wave crests and crashes down into the culture, however, skepticism such as mine seems likely to grow rarer. Pressure will build to embrace unreservedly the convenience and efficiency of workerless restaurants, automated factories, networked appliances, facial-recognition technology, virtual personal assistants, and all the rest. Standing apart from it will take uncommon fortitude. Who will want to be left behind by the glorious and liberated future being dreamed up for all by the techdaddy visionaries of Silicon Valley?

Don't answer; it's a rhetorical question. The glorious future won't leave anyone behind because it won't be optional. You will be forced to participate whether you want to or not. The logic of the marketplace and the natural human desire for sparkly things will carry you along on the irresistible tide of a faster, better, cheaper, and digitally optimized consumer experience. Your new dishwasher will want to talk to your Amazon Echo. Your new car will get annoyed if it can't communicate with the map app on your telephone. Your Fitbit will have a relationship with your coffee machine and your popcorn popper. They'll all be sending reports back to Palo Alto or Mountain View or Cupertino. Try finding an old-fashioned phone for sale these days, or a television that isn't rigged out with a digital amygdala. You can probably do it, but only if you commit an amount of time rivaling that which you'd devote to child-rearing or some other full-time job. The work of dodging the digitalization of everything will become harder and harder. Pockets of resistance will be colonized and converted. Holdouts will be ostracized. You will comply.

Everyone has at least one friend who promised never to use Facebook, only to relent once he realized he couldn't make dinner reservations without it. Eventually everyone succumbs to the siren song of Silicon Valley. Eventually we all decide it's easier to go along with what seem like minor changes to the way we live than it is to fight them. We draw a line in the sand only to rub it out and draw another one. Then, one day, we wake up and Elon Musk and Mark Zuckerberg are paying us not to work.

Think I'm too pessimistic? Think I'm scaremongering? Think big social changes don't swing that quickly? Ask the Luddites how it worked out for them. Ask the thousands of newspaper reporters and editors who've lost their jobs in the past decade because of the self-negating proposition that information wants to be free.[11] Ask the immigrant cab drivers who worked for decades to buy their very own New York City taxi medallions only to see their investments practically vaporized in a few years by the ride-sharing revolution. Ask the millions of young Americans who'll be robbed of a first job on the bottom rung of the economic ladder in the next few years because of automation. Ask the millions of Americans who've already lost hope that the economy will ever work again for them during their lifetimes and so have turned to nationalism, Trumpism, or opioids to satisfy their deep yearnings for a life worth living, or at the very least a life without psychic pain.

I'm merely taking seriously what the techdaddies are promising, and observing how the 80 million-plus millennials are reacting to those promises. My warnings about the changes I see are more arithmetic than they are alarmism. Silicon Valley has been asking millennials, "Do you want to live this way?" and the answer has been a resounding "Yeah!" Just to be sure, the techdaddies are spelling it out: "We are going to digitize everything, give most of your jobs to robots, double your

---

11 Hennessey's theorem: The freer information is, the less of it there will be.

lifespan, colonize other planets, and put you on permanent welfare. The only things you will lose are the things we have been training you not to care about: privacy, freedom of speech, humor, and the annoyances of having to interact with others when you want to buy a shirt or fill a prescription. You still in?"

"Hell yeah!"

The purpose of this book has been to remind you that the analog, brick-and-mortar, flesh-and-blood world that formed me, you, and everyone over the age of 40 had many virtues; chief among them was the chance to be what you were—namely a human being who enjoyed living alongside and in contact with other human beings. Fifty-four percent of millennials told *TIME* researchers that they were more comfortable texting people than talking with them. A May 2017 Harris Poll found that 36 percent of millennials felt that emojis, GIFs, and stickers used to enhance text and instant messaging were more useful than words for expressing emotion. A shocking (to this Gen Xer) 68 percent of millennials said they were "more comfortable" using visual aids than they were talking on the telephone.

These are statistics that portend a very particular kind of doom. In the digital world, as we all have learned to our dismay in recent years, it's too easy to throw anonymous stones. It's too easy to misread the intent behind an e-mail or a text. There's no subtlety. Nuances, where they exist, are all but impossible to discern. Everybody always interprets things in the most aggressive and uncharitable lights. People who communicate only via e-mail and text are apt to misunderstand each other with greater frequency than pals who chat face-to-face, or even over the telephone.

And then there is the isolation. Have you seen the young couple in the restaurant who are on a date but have their heads buried in their devices? There are few sights as depressing. Have you seen the family out for a trip to the zoo or the beach who can't get junior to put down his iPhone? That's not happiness and harmony. We are headed toward a zombified social dystopia in which people would rather interact with others online than in person. That's not a good direction for us to go.

The meaning of personal responsibility has already been diluted by ubiquitous social media, the app-based sharing economy, and the impersonal Internet of Things. The ethos of anonymous insults, mob justice, and public shaming rules us now the way a drug rules an addict.

Gossip, smears, rumors, lies, and threats proliferate like mushrooms on the Internet forest floor. Trolls bait strangers into Twitter wars. The conditions for social conflict are optimal. Is it a coincidence that the 2016 presidential campaign was the most scandal-ridden, bottom-feeding, anxiety-inducing election in living memory? Is there any doubt that the Twitter presidency will be a permanent, and toxic, feature of the rest of our lives? Who among us would choose to go to high school now, during the era of the naked selfie, the relationship status update, and the disappearing Snapchat? I'd guess there aren't many who'd volunteer.

It doesn't have to be this way. There was a time when Facebook, Twitter, Instagram, Snapchat, Uber, Tinder, Apple, Google, and Amazon didn't exist. There was a time when no one thought it an advantage to be able to check yourself out of the grocery store without the aid of a human clerk. There was a time when friendships depended on personal intimacy of the sort that an emoji just doesn't convey. There was a time when the phone rang and everyone in the house got excited. There was a time when asking someone out on a date required courage. There was a time when no American in his right mind believed that words and ideas could hurt you just the same as sticks and stones. There was a time when young people kicked back hard at anyone who suggested that certain forms of political and artistic expression ought to be censored.

If you're about my age, you remember that time, though it may seem very far away and inaccessible to you now. It's actually not that far away, and not that inaccessible. The technology that we use to communicate, socialize, and buy stuff is all—still—only about 10 years old. Unless you were an early adopter, you probably first learned to rely on these things relatively recently. You can unlearn your reliance on them. We all can.

But how? That's the $64,000 question, if indeed the bounty on big questions is still only $64,000. Whatever the price, big questions rarely have easy answers. Depending on how eager you are for me to offer a grand Gen X philosophy or a concrete program of political action and spiritual renewal, you may not find what I'm about to spell out terribly satisfying. If you've read the previous chapters, you probably have inferred a lot of it anyway.

It amounts to this: put down the phone. That's the most consequential thing you can do. In 2017, more than three-quarters of Americans owned an Internet-enabled smartphone. That was up from just 35 percent in 2011. If you subtract the elderly, the toddlers, and the incarcerated, basically everyone now has a smartphone. We've seen what it's doing to high school and college students, isolating them socially and robbing them of their ability to concentrate. It's having the same effect on middle-aged folks like you and me. Whether it's something as seemingly benign as digital distraction during Saturday morning pancakes or something as dangerous as the widespread habit of texting while driving, we all are hooked like fish on a string. We all need to put down the phones and learn to leave them down. Most of us, myself included, waste dozens upon dozens of hours every week on the empty calories of social media and mostly pointless web surfing. It's unproductive, habit-forming behavior. It sets a bad example for our kids and we'd be better off not doing it. Even Steve Jobs wouldn't let his children use an iPhone or an iPad.

This will be hardest for millennials. They simply have not been groomed for a life that doesn't involve near-constant smartphone usage. So Gen Xers need to lead, and do so visibly. Take the initiative. You will not die if you put your phone away for a few days. Your career will not end. Your kids will not drown. Everything will be okay. It may even be better. You may find that you can think again, like you used to. You may find you can talk with people, eye to eye, without scrolling your social-media feed while they are speaking. You may find you can relate again to the people around you in a compassionate way. You may find that you smile more. You may meet and speak with more people, making more friends in the process. You may find you are more forgiving of those who disagree with you about politics and other seemingly important things. You may find you no longer see something happening and think, "This will make a great post."

Try it. See what happens. I doubt you'll be disappointed. And if it doesn't work, you can always go back to the way you've been doing things. This phone technology and social-media stuff isn't going anywhere. Trust me on that.

Here's something else you can do: pay for the entertainment you consume. The books, movies, TV shows, and music you like don't grow on trees. The artists and writers who produce them will produce less of them if they don't get paid for their efforts. Music pirating of the Napster sort is no longer the problem it was 15 years ago, but only because most artists' songs and albums can now be found on YouTube for free. Unless they or their representatives are dogged about tracking down and shutting down copyright violations, artists have to live with a certain amount of what they produce getting ripped off. In some cases they've simply given up and posted their entire catalogs online.

I've done it, I won't sit here and lie; I've listened to entire albums on YouTube rather than buying a copy for myself. I've watched movies and television shows that way as well. But it isn't right. I know it isn't right and you do, too. The adult thing to do is to act on those pangs of conscience and stop doing it altogether. When you hear a song on the old-fashioned terrestrial radio, the artist gets paid. Same when you listen on Spotify or Pandora or a subscription service like Amazon Music or Apple Music (though these services don't pay much). But if you just grab it off YouTube, the artist probably gets nothing or next to nothing. That's not a sustainable model. Nor is it fair. You and I both know that it's having a deleterious effect on the music business, and to a lesser extent the film business. Pay for what you consume.

Visiting a brick-and-mortar store and helping the real economy survive the online onslaught is a noble choice. Increasingly, however, it's a choice you can't make even if you want to. Retail is doomed. The department stores, record stores, video-rental stores, non-chain book stores, and little independent movie theaters we grew up with are for the most part gone. They aren't coming back. If you must buy things like movies, music, and books over the Internet, try to buy directly from the artists themselves, the ones responsible for producing the stuff in the first place. Look around. Most musicians sell CDs and MP3s directly to their fans via their websites. Authors sometimes do this, too, or will provide a link that helps them to make a little more off their hard work than they would get if you simply ordered the book through one of the big online sites. You can even buy DVDs from independent filmmakers if you like their stuff. Cut out the middle man. It sends a clear message about what you value and what you don't, and it represents a nice handful of sand in the gears of the giant jealous corporations that would like you to dance only with them in their walled gardens forever.

Subscribe to a newspaper and a few magazines if you can afford to, hopefully because you like them and feel they provide you with something you need and can't get anywhere else. But even if you are ambivalent about the form that your news consumption takes, recognize that reporting, writing, and editing stories is a costly business. The media isn't always perfect or right, but it's a damn good thing we have one. That industry has already shrunk to a shadow of its former self. I don't think our democracy will be well served if it shrinks much further.

Consolidations, mergers, and bankruptcies have sapped the print news media of the variety and perspective that once made it an invaluable counterweight to the behemoth, corporate news that predominated on television—and to the official government line. If you value good reporting, you should contribute to it. If you don't subscribe to newspapers, they will go away, and your children will have nothing to read except Facebook GIFs, Twitter memes, and idiotic BuzzFeed hot takes. It's hard for me to believe that Gen Xers would prefer to live in a world without daily newspapers in the driveway and weekly magazines on the newsstand, but that world is coming—unless you, me, and all our friends are willing to put a few bucks into the effort to forestall it.

Resist the Internet of Things, reject utopian Silicon Valley promises, and raise your children to view the online world as a place to visit, not to live. This is where the battle will really be won. Don't give your kids cell phones on the first day of kindergarten. Let them learn to live without the digital umbilical cord. Give them room to roam and develop away from Silicon Valley's prying eyes. Keep them off the Internet for as long as you can. Children need exposure to risk. They need alone time and they need to learn how to wait. They need to learn how to read, how to think, and how not to be checking their social media feeds every 90 seconds.

Remember David McCullough's words:

Information is important. Information is valuable. It can be worth a lot of money. It can be decisive in which direction one goes in one's life or which direction a country goes, but it isn't learning. I like to tell students: "If you memorized *The World Almanac*, you would not be learned. You would be weird." No computer ever yet has had an idea. They only happen here, in the human brain, in the human imagination.

The Internet has no imagination, no brain, no heart, and no soul, and like a resentful lover it has decided that we shouldn't have these things, either. The Internet gives us access to all the information we could ever need, but it takes away our ability to think for ourselves and remember what we've learned. It gives us the illusion of connection, but it erodes our actual ability to connect with other people face to face. Perhaps even worse, it takes away our desire to do these things. Like a codependent relative, the Internet demands our attention at all times and in all circumstances. "The experience of losing our Internet connection becomes more and more like losing a friend," said the authors of that *Science Magazine* report on memory. "We must remain plugged in to know what Google knows."

This coming technium, which we can see emerging in the already disrupted industries—the news media, transportation, retail, advertising—and in corners of the culture where young people gather, is tailor-made for the millennial mindset. The day will soon be here when every industry adopts Silicon Valley's youth obsession—35 and out. Even as Gen Xers approach our fifties, an age once considered to be a person's prime working years, we are in many workplaces potentially en route to redundancy.

You may expect me to advocate the Luddite solution to this problem. You might expect me to call on Gen X to smash the digital looms or lay our bodies across the proverbial gears, insisting upon the de-Internetification of the economy. But it's not so simple as beat 'em or join 'em. I happen to think there is a third way—tell 'em to slow this bad boy down. We are moving way too fast toward the techdaddies' dreamworld and we need to pump the brakes. The baby boomers don't seem interested in doing it. The millennials are too green to realize the dangers. The job falls to Generation X.

Do not go quietly into the good night of millennial domination, whether in your professional or personal life. Stand up for regular order, face-to-face meetings, and systems that reward merit over all else. Celebrate experience. Find a way to promote humanistic values. Don't let childish ignorance or the promise of a utopian future steamroll your sense of right and wrong. Give as good as you get, even as the grey hairs form on your temple, as technological change outpaces your ability—and desire—to keep up, and your 20/20 vision begins to blur. Gen X may be small, but we are tough. Our specific experiences should allow us to punch above our weight.

It's zero hour. Don't just stand there. Bust a move.

ACKNOWLEDGMENTS

This book was written in transit. The Metro-North Railroad made it possible for me to live in the suburbs and work in New York City. It also made it possible for me to write *Zero Hour for Gen X* when it eliminated the famous bar cars in 2014 and enforced silence in the quiet cars starting in 2016. The former was a source of occasional distraction; the latter a daily refuge.

I would like to thank Margi Conklin for running my Gen X piece in the Sunday *New York Post* and kicking this thing off. Mary Kissel and Rush Limbaugh offered unsolicited encouragement at critical stages of the development of the idea. My competent and patriotic millennial colleagues on the editorial features staff of the *Wall Street Journal* remind me daily that not every member of their generation deserves scorn. Kyle Peterson, Cori O'Connor, Mene Ukueberuwa, and Jason Willick inspire hope that all is not yet lost. Adam O'Neal especially deserves acknowledgment for drawing my attention to the Maxine Waters remark leading off Chapter One. I'm eternally grateful to Paul Gigot and James Taranto for their confidence.

I'm indebted to the Manhattan Institute's Larry Mone, Vanessa Mendoza, and Leigh Harrington for their support over the years. Bernadette Serton patiently answered elementary questions about how book deals get made. Jamie Meggas took my photo.

My friends at *City Journal* helped move my "thesis" from daydream to the page. Brian Anderson agreed to publish the earliest version online and graciously allowed me the space to develop the idea in print. Michele Jacob got the message right away and helped tell the world. Harry Stein's strategic advice was crucial. Steve Malanga has always treated me as a peer, which is unjustifiable, and Paul Beston read early versions of the manuscript. His encouragement kept me going, and his friendship is a boon.

The Encounter Books crew got me over the finish line and helped me navigate the unfamiliar world of publishing. I'm thinking specifically of Sam Schneider, Lauren Miklos, Caitlin Kiley, Katherine Wong, and Super Copy Editors. There would of course be no *Zero Hour* without Roger Kimball's say-so.

My late father-in-law, Bill Reel, was the first to suggest that I could make a living by slinging words on a page. He gave me more than a career, though; he gave me his only daughter, Ursula, to have and to hold. How can you thank a man for that?

I would like to thank my father, Jim Hennessey, for all his love and support and for showing me what it means to be a good man. There's no way I can think of to express what my wife and children have done to inspire and sustain me. I'll simply say this: All of my tomorrows belong to you.

INDEX